"We are living in a deeply divisive time when our American democracy is in jeopardy. During this reality, Chuck Mingo and Troy Jackson have provided a path forward in *Living Undivided*. This book is an invitation to freedom rooted in love and justice. If you want to build a new future together with others in a world that desperately needs change, this book is for you! I highly recommend it!"

Dr. Brenda Salter McNeil, author of *Becoming Brave* and *Roadmap to Reconciliation 2.0*

"Amid the millions who marched for Black lives and those who pushed back with campaigns against critical race theory, Chuck Mingo and Troy Jackson have worked faithfully with thousands of real people who were willing to listen to one another, trusting the Spirit to make a way toward beloved community. *Living Undivided* is the fruit of that work, offered as a feast for all who hunger and thirst for justice."

Jonathan Wilson-Hartgrove, author of *Revolution of Values*

"Justice is not peripheral but intrinsic to the gospel, and today it's critical to its advance. Indeed, an increasingly diverse society no longer finds credible a message of God's love for all people as proclaimed from segregated pulpits and pews that perpetuate racialized fatigue, harm, and trauma. In *Living Undivided*, Chuck and Troy do more than opine the 'why we should' of Christian unity. They share experientially forged, proven, and practical 'what to do and how to do it' insights that will equip and challenge you to walk, work, and worship God together as one with others, beyond the distinctions that otherwise divide this world. More than a good read, it's a great game plan."

"It is obvious that racial tensions are real in our country. Therefore, it is important to have more discussion and more perspectives shared. Chuck and Troy enter dangerous waters to throw us a lifeline."

"At this troubled moment in America comes this brilliant book to remind us that unconditional love has the power to heal and to bind us together across the divides of race and faith. Chuck and Troy have brought us to the altar of racial healing and baptized us in the waters of radical love—a love that conveys hard truths, asks and answers tough questions, and allows us to lament and learn to live together. Amen!"

"This deeply moving book is a fierce invitation to engagement that is smart, rooted, and courageous, moving toward a renewed, restored society of justice."

LIVING UNDIVIDED

LOVING COURAGEOUSLY FOR
RACIAL HEALING AND JUSTICE

CHUCK MINGO AND **TROY JACKSON**
WITH HOLLY CRAWSHAW

BakerBooks

a division of Baker Publishing Group
Grand Rapids, Michigan

Published by Baker Books
a division of Baker Publishing Group
Grand Rapids, Michigan
BakerBooks.com

Printed in the United States of America

Library of Congress Cataloging-in-Publication Data
Names: Mingo, Chuck, 1976– author. | Jackson, Troy, 1968– author.
Title: Living undivided : loving courageously for racial healing and justice / Chuck Mingo and Troy Jackson.
Description: Grand Rapids : Baker Books, a division of Baker Publishing Group, [2023] | Includes bibliographical references.
Identifiers: LCCN 2022024780 | ISBN 9781540902283 (cloth) | ISBN 9781493439560 (ebook)
Subjects: LCSH: Racism—Religious aspects—Christianity. | Race relations—Religious aspects—Christianity. | Reconciliation—Religious aspects—Christianity. | Interpersonal relations—Religious aspects—Christianity. | Christianity and justice. | Love—Religious aspects—Christianity.
Classification: LCC BT734.2 .M56 2023 | DDC 241/.675—dc23/eng/20220701
LC record available at https://lccn.loc.gov/2022024780

The authors are represented by The Fedd Agency, Inc.

Baker Publishing Group publications use paper produced from sustainable forestry practices and post-consumer waste whenever possible.

24   25   26   27   28   29   30   7   6   5   4   3   2   1

From Chuck:
to Maria, Nathan, Samuel, and Isabel

From Troy:
to Amanda, Jacob, Emma, and Ellie

To Holly Crawshaw:
You were instrumental in this book being written.
Thanks for being a wise, patient,
and encouraging writing partner.
We are so thankful for you.

CONTENTS

Foreword   9

Note to Readers   15

Introduction   17

PART 1: ROOT   39

1. Chuck's Story   47

2. Troy's Story   65

PART 2: REALIZE   87

3. Hope in History   91

4. Stagnant Roots   105

5. Two Empowering Commitments   127

PART 3: RESPOND   143

6. The Power of Community   149

PART 4: RECKON   159

7. The Faithful Path   163

PART 5: RESTORE   183

8. Power Supply   187

9. What Does the Lord Require of You?   195

PART 6: RESOLVE   209

10. Everyday Courage   213

Epilogue: A Call to Living Undivided   225

Acknowledgments   229

Notes   233

About the Authors   237

FOREWORD

by Dave Ferguson

Nearly forty years ago, I went on a two-week mission trip to Haiti, an experience that became a spiritual reckoning. Seeing that level of poverty firsthand was as eye-opening as it was distressing. Racism is a defining characteristic of Haitian society, and it was a kick to the soul to witness its malignancy in the lives of Haiti's poorest families and children.

There was this guy in our group from a different church named Troy Jackson. Troy stood out to me because he asked all the tough questions out loud that I was wrestling with internally. I wanted to get to know him. So I did.

The following summer, Troy came to Chicago to visit. While in town, a few of us attended a Kool & The Gang concert. I'll save you the Google search and tell you that you've already danced to their biggest hit, "Celebration," at a family member's wedding. "Celebrate good times, come on!" Yes, that's Kool & The Gang.

Somehow, between ministry and jamming out to funk, Troy and I forged a bond. God allowed our paths to intersect again a few years later. We were both headed on mission trips to different parts of the world, but we met up in Miami. I asked Troy to do an internship at Community Christian Church—a church I was planting in a suburb of Chicago. I don't know if it was Troy's great taste in music, the draw of his insatiable curiosity, or a prophetic nudge from God, but I knew he was a man I wanted to continue to learn from.

And for the last three and a half decades, that's exactly what I've done. I've had a front-row seat to Troy's quest to answer the same question he asked in Haiti: Why racism? He's become one of the first people I tap to talk about issues relating to racial justice or civil rights. Troy pushes me. He challenges me. And he coaches me. Troy is the person I call and ask, "Hey, what do I need to know about this issue? How should I think about this?" Because I trust his research, his heart, and his integrity that much.

Another great gift my friendship with Troy has given me is Chuck Mingo. I first met Chuck at the 2018 Exponential Conference. Chuck did most of the talking. I immediately felt a connection. As I got to know him, I discovered that he brought a rare combination of gifts: a passion for racial solidarity, a results mindset, and a world-class ability to communicate in front of a small group, a camera, or an audience of thousands. Plus, Chuck is just a really good guy!

From my vantage point, especially when it comes to addressing our perpetual racial challenges in this nation and the church, you can't find more knowledgeable, passionate, or Bible-minded people than Troy and Chuck and their team.

I wasn't surprised when Chuck and Troy combined their skill sets and passions to launch an organization called UNDIVIDED, a movement for racial healing, solidarity, and justice. One of the encounters hosted by the organization is called LivingUNDI-VIDED—a seven-session journey where they get people together in mixed-race groups to share their stories and perspectives. After walking more than ten thousand people through their LivingUNDIVIDED journey, Troy and Chuck have inspired countless others to make a difference in their communities.

It wasn't long after UNDIVIDED started that I found myself with a problem and Chuck and Troy were the solution. The fall after George Floyd's murder, I helped plan about one hundred roundtable events across the country for church leaders to come together to discuss racial reconciliation and solidarity. While I knew how to deliver content in a roundtable setting, I didn't know how to create meaningful conversations on race and racism in such a polarizing time. I had the proverbial cart in front of the horse!

So, with a few thousand leaders ready to come to these roundtables, my need was significant. Chuck and Troy assured me that with their combined experience through UNDIVIDED, they could facilitate meaningful discussions between those church leaders. And they totally delivered.

Over the last couple of years, my relationships with Chuck and Troy have become more important to me than ever. As a country, we've watched in heartache and horror as the stories of Breonna Taylor, Ahmaud Arbery, George Floyd, and countless others have unfolded, stirring Americans to ask the same questions Troy asked in Haiti in the mid-1980s.

After my own small group participated in the LivingUNDI-VIDED experience, I remember looking around to see a room full of Black, Brown, Asian Pacific Islander, and White people. The White participants looked exhausted yet eager. They'd had their eyes opened. They had been challenged to the core of who they were. But the People of Color in the room spoke up and said, "Hey, what's been a chapter in your life has been our entire story."

It was a moment that solidified our commitment to the UNDIVIDED organization. In fact, the experience was so powerful, we have now held multiple cohorts and hope to lead our entire church through the LivingUNDIVIDED experience.

One moment I will never forget from the experience was something my longtime friend Eddie said to me. During the weeks we were together, eight Asian Pacific Islander women were murdered in the city of Atlanta in a tragic mass shooting. Eddie is from a Korean background. As we were processing what happened in our LivingUNDIVIDED group that night, Eddie said something that may be the most poignant moment of our relationship. He looked at me and said, "I wish this made you angrier."

It took a lot of courage on his part to say this, and it struck a deep chord within me. Eddie's words reminded me that this fight was personal for all of us, because the impacts of racism were deeply wounding my dear friend. It moved me from being intellectually opposed to racial injustice to being emotionally engaged. Eddie's courage moved the work from my head to my heart—and I'm so grateful for that.

I pray this happens for each of you as you read this book.

Addressing racism is hard. It's weighty. You may not feel like an expert. I'm not sure anyone does. But as leaders, we must create space for what's important—and taking a stance on injustice is critical. It's vital to the church at large, and it's important to God.

The root of why some of us avoid initiating conversations or leading others on race is fear. That fear is standing between us and realizing God's dream of racial unity and peace. That fear is robbing us of a richer life experience. That fear is limiting our spiritual growth. Second Timothy 1:7 says, "For God did not give us a spirit of cowardice but rather a spirit of power and of love and of self-discipline."

We may feel incapable on our own, but God in us is capable. Through God, we have the authority and ability to participate in and facilitate these crucial conversations on race and justice. So lean in with the power, love, and self-discipline given to you through God's Holy Spirit. Combine God's gifts to you with the messages in this book and link arms with your brothers and sisters in Christ, moving closer to God's intention for his people.

When I think about why UNDIVIDED is really important, I come right back to the gospel. My understanding of the gospel is that Jesus is King, and he has a kingdom, and his kingdom doesn't look like I do. It looks like a diverse group of people all coming together, worshiping him. In fact, that's exactly what's described in Revelation 7:9, where it talks about a gathering of people from every tongue, tribe, and nation. The UNDIVIDED movement draws us closer to God's dream.

Racial solidarity is possible. But not without our full participation. I encourage you to read this book with an open mind and a soft heart. You may have to reexamine some long-held viewpoints and philosophies. You may even have to realign and adjust some of your theology. In fact, I hope you do.

As you continue your LivingUNDIVIDED journey, I pray that you have an encounter with Jesus's courageous love—a love with the power to change us. A love with the power to heal us.

NOTE TO READERS

Throughout our time together, we will be using words, phrases, and capitalization to describe groups of people, movements, and organizations. We have applied research and consulted with others to choose our words and usage both carefully and intentionally.

Unless otherwise noted, we will be using the following terminology to describe certain races and ethnicities:

Asian Pacific Islander
Black
Brown
Indigenous
Latin American
People of Color
White

We will also use the term Black, Indigenous, and People of Color (BIPOC for short) to describe these people groups collectively.

Language is fluid, changing over time, and often contested. In our use of terms, we strive for sensitivity and accuracy for our readers and to be guided by the Holy Spirit.

INTRODUCTION

Did you know that an Apple Watch will automatically call 911 if it detects that the wearer's heart rate is unusually high? I (Chuck) discovered this feature during an early morning run while crossing a bridge.

It was a warm summer morning, and the sun had just risen over the Ohio River. Glazed in perspiration, I was feeling that "runner's high" as I was out that day with my good friend Chris—that is, until we approached a bridge. As we started across the narrow path on the edge of the bridge, to quote Eminem, it was a "Yo! His palms are sweaty, knees weak, arms are heavy" moment.[1] And then as I was already feeling that flip-floppy, woozy, reeling thing that happens when you're on the brink of something that scares you, my watch and phone started barking at me. When I looked down to check what was wrong, I saw that after detecting my elevated heart rate, my watch had automatically dialed 911 . . . and the operator had picked up the call! After an awkward conversation that added embarrassment to fear, I knew it was a run, and an Apple Watch feature, I wouldn't soon forget.

I've been a runner for over a decade, and still, every time I cross a bridge, it causes my pace to quicken and my heart to pound. Fear is like that, right? It's emotional. It's visceral. Fear grips your heart.

Today, when I think about how folks across the country are feeling about race, often the predominant emotion is fear. Whether it's the fear of being harmed, the fear of being canceled for speaking up or speaking out, or the fear that the racial divisions will tear our communities apart, the gravity of fear continues to hold us down.

If our society wore an Apple Watch, it would have been calling 911 every single day since the murder of George Floyd in 2020 sparked another racial reckoning in our country.

Yet, while George Floyd's murder was a keystone event, as history demonstrates, it was not the first. I serve on the pastoral team at Crossroads Church, a large multisite church of more than thirty-five thousand people, in Cincinnati, Ohio. In 2015, our church demographics were about 80 percent White and 20 percent Black, Indigenous, and People of Color. On July 19 of that year, body cam footage from a traffic stop just five miles from where I pastored showed the tragic last moments of the life of Samuel DuBose.

A White University of Cincinnati officer pulled over DuBose, a Black motorist, for a missing front license plate. Their exchange ended with the officer firing his gun, killing DuBose.

When local news stations broadcasted the body cam video, I joined a few of my colleagues to watch. As the only Black man in the room, I felt both in community and also alone. In community because Crossroads is a church that cares about changing the world. We were growing in diversity and being intentional about our staff and volunteers reflecting the makeup of the community. And yet I also felt strangely alone. Why? It was because as I watched the footage, as a Black man and a pastor, I felt a special weight of responsibility that was unavoidable and would require something unique from me.

I knew no one else in that room, as well-intentioned and heartbroken as they were, would be taking the mantle to lead our church in this time of crisis and division. Not because they didn't care deeply (they did), and not because they weren't qualified (some were more qualified than me), but because *God was calling me*. But this calling came with that bridge-crossing kind of fear that much was at stake. As I discerned how to lead our community well in this moment, the weight made my heart sink to the pit of my stomach.

I was standing at the edge of the longest, highest bridge I'd ever crossed. I had a choice to make. Would I allow fear to keep me stagnant, or would I move forward, flowing toward racial healing, solidarity, and justice by taking a more active role in the struggle?

I chose to move forward. I chose to step into the struggle and allow my position and leadership to become a conduit for the flow of racial healing and justice that God was birthing in me and in our church.

Not surprisingly, there was a divided interpretation of the facts of that deadly traffic stop and whether a church should be talking about it. Flowing meant teaching and preaching honestly about racism, its spiritual roots, and its impact in our community. It was showing up at marches in my city to be a prayerful and faithful presence with others crying out for justice. It meant following brave lay leaders in my church like Carolyn and Elizabeth, who organized a "Jericho prayer walk" with hundreds of people seeking a just outcome in the case of the officer who shot and killed Samuel DuBose. It meant leading prayer outside the justice center as the jury deliberated amid a fraught and potentially explosive environment.

Why was it important to show up in the middle of such tension? Because in the Gospels, this is where we find Jesus over and over again. Jesus chose to be with those most affected by the injustice in his day, chose to stand in the gap, chose to be present where there was pain. In order for our lives to be touched by the lasting racial healing and justice that flows from the throne of God, we must make the same choice—to stand with those most affected by racial injustice. This is what it means to live undivided.

See, this isn't another book on racism in America.

Okay, so this isn't *just* another book on racism in America. This is a book about you. About your life, your walk with God, and your future. This book is also about us, together—about our shared future. This is also a book rooted not only in ideas but also experience through ongoing action in congregations, organizations, and communities.

We believe that pursuing racial healing and justice is a shared project of fierce love and humility that requires all of us.

This book is about how we can be a "sign of coming attractions" of the picture God painted of the kingdom in Revelation 7:9—a picture created with strokes of many glorious colors, a picture of joy and justice and human flourishing. We're inviting you to get into the flow for racial healing and justice that God is already bringing about through his people—a flow of fresh water into the dead sea of society.

This book is an invitation to all.

This book is a challenge to all.

We're inviting and challenging you to come alive in the story of racial healing and justice that God is writing. We're calling you out of the isolating and parched desert of fear with an invitation to step into the life-giving flow with us. Why? Because we've seen the life-changing results of thousands upon thousands of people coming alive to this invitation and challenge, beginning with the two of us.

UNDIVIDED Is Born

I (Chuck) met Troy in the atrium of my church. Within the first few minutes, this White guy told me he just got back from marching in an event to elevate the life and experiences of Black people in Ferguson, Missouri. Immediately, he shook all the preconceived notions I had about him. But I still didn't know him.

Minutes into this first conversation, he asked me these intense questions about how I felt about race, policing, and faith. I was thinking, *Dude, we just met. I don't know you, and I certainly don't know if I can trust you with how I'm really feeling about all this.* I gave Troy "safe" answers to his questions, refusing to let down my guard. Have you ever responded that way when the topic of race entered the conversation? Then Troy told me his story—which was filled with examples of his work for the cause of racial solidarity—further dismantling the wall I'd had to build around myself as a Person of Color in a conversation with a White man.

I don't know if he said enough for me to realize he was genuinely invested or if I was just thankful for the opportunity to unload some of the internal tension I was feeling, but the next thing I knew, I was sharing honestly with Troy that I felt like we were back in the 1960s. I told him I felt called to do something but didn't know what that looked like.

Troy extended an invitation to me to get involved with the racial justice organization he was leading, which I accepted. A few months later, as the vision for UNDIVIDED was birthed in me, I invited Troy to be part of building something that could draw followers of Jesus to the work of racial healing, solidarity, and justice—just like his conversation had done for me.

Along with Lynn Watts, Troy and I formed a diverse team of leaders to create UNDIVIDED, a seven-session experiential journey for multiracial groups of people to pursue racial solidarity and justice. Each week, we root ourselves in the Bible and draw deeper into relationships and mutual understanding through group conversations, activities, and assignments. The journey fosters belonging, hope, deep community, and faithful action.

As the program was growing in our church, we saw thousands of people connecting, lowering their defenses, and taking action.

Then 2020 came: a contentious election; a pandemic; dehumanizing rhetoric and violence against Asian Pacific Islander and immigrant communities; and the tragic killings of more Black and Brown people caught on video, including Ahmaud Arbery at the hands of two brazen citizens. It all added up to more pain. More division. More fear.

The events of 2020 also caused us to reexamine how the UNDIVIDED experience was serving the vision of racial healing and justice. God brought two incredible Black leaders, Brittany Wade and Courtney Walton, to our UNDIVIDED leadership team. Brittany is nationally known for her research on the intersection of race and faith, including findings on the effectiveness of programs like UNDIVIDED. Courtney is pursuing an EdD in the impact of race-based trauma. Guided by the two of them, we made significant enhancements to our content and experiences, and the results have been fruitful. What began as a program in one church has expanded across the country. It's a catalyst for not only activating communities into the work of justice but also encouraging the kind of deep and powerful healing needed to sustain healthy cross-racial communities.

We're seeing people faithfully heed God's call for racial healing and justice. Social scientists have validated the effectiveness of our UNDIVIDED experiences, and we've witnessed the transformative stories of communities and individuals, some which you will hear in the pages that follow. Our journey also includes the messiness and imperfections that come with every effort to address something as complex as racism.

We talk a lot about loving courageously in this book, because unity over fear is possible. It takes *courage* to get to know—*to care about*—other people and other lived experiences that make up our churches and our nation. We will also talk about our mistakes, because this work requires humility and a willingness to "fail forward" toward meaningful outcomes.

This is how hearts change.

If you picked up this book, it's likely you desire racial healing and justice to flow as well, and you want to discover and do your part to bring it about. Like you, we've been troubled by the stories of racial injustice and division that mark these times. We understand how it feels to want to make a difference but to be unsure or unclear of the role you're called to play. We wrote this book to be a road map for you. God is at work healing and restoring those affected by the chronic disease of racism. This book is an invitation for you to join God in this sacred work.

An Animating Vision

As you start the journey with us, we want to share the biblical vision that animates the UNDIVIDED movement. These theological convictions undergird everything you will read in this book. As pastors and followers of Jesus, we want our passion for and picture of what Jesus called the kingdom of God (the reign of God) to be at the heart of our work.

The Launch Party for the Church

One of the special experiences we have had in our lives was the opportunity to visit Israel and be on the land where Bible stories took place. One of my (Chuck's) favorite memories happened in Bethlehem at a small chapel called Shepherds' Field, where some suggest the angels visited the shepherds to announce the birth of Jesus as chronicled in the Gospel of Luke.

As is true at many sites in Israel connected to Scripture, we were surrounded by Jesus followers from all walks of life and from all over the world. There we all were, on a hot day in the Middle East, converging on this sacred site. Dozens of different languages were being spoken simultaneously, all of us united in excitement, awe, and wonder to be in the "little town of Bethlehem." Another common thing about the churches in Israel is that they have great acoustics! So, not surprisingly, when people are in the Shepherds' Field chapel, they sing Christmas carols.

Most groups have enough people to fill the small chapel themselves, so each group waits patiently for their turn to go into the chapel and sing. However, when we arrived, the group ahead of us wasn't large and the people were clearly from another nation and didn't speak or sing in English. Their priest shared a brief reflection in their language, then invited them to sing a familiar tune, "O Come, All Ye Faithful." When they got to the chorus, the priest looked at me and gestured for us to join in. So there we were, in the middle of Israel, sharing a moment of common worship of a common God. And though we didn't share the same language, we were able to share the same song.

This is a picture of God's intent for the church. There's something special about experiencing the multiethnic, multicultural, multihued church of Jesus together. The fact that our country is so racially divided and yet the church is designed to live undivided means there's a God-sized opportunity. From Genesis to Revelation, we see that God is about the work of gathering to himself a new family made of people from every nation.

Early in the book of Acts, we read how God's Spirit empowered the apostles to speak languages they had never learned so more people could become followers of Jesus. What began in the earliest days of Christianity as recorded in Acts 2 comes to full fruition in Revelation 7:9, when John had a vision that every language, every tongue, every nation, every tribe of people was gathered in unity and celebration at the throne of God.

These were people who had distinct ethnicities and languages but were united as one at the throne of God. They may not have shared the same language, but they shared the same song—one of joy and gratitude to the God who has, as it says in Colossians 1:20, reconciled "to himself all things."

One New Humanity

This animating vision is also seen in the second chapter of Paul's letter to the Ephesian church. We love Ephesians 2:1–10, where Paul describes how we are reconciled with God. He stresses that we are saved by grace and not by anything we can do for ourselves. We cannot boast. It's not about us. It's all about what Jesus did on our behalf. Then in Ephesians 2:14–15, Paul describes the miracle of unity made possible by Jesus:

> For he [Jesus] is our peace; in his flesh he has made both into one and has broken down the dividing wall, that is, the hostility between us, abolishing the law with its commandments and ordinances, that he might create in himself one new humanity in place of the two, thus making peace.

Through Jesus, we become one new humanity. Paul is responding to a very real division in the early church: the split between Jew and gentile. This was a conflict along ethnic and cultural lines rooted in the political tensions of the day in the Roman Empire. Sound familiar? The new identity and community Jesus ushered in was not bound by partisan political divisions or ethnic and racial differences. The early church embraced becoming one new humanity because they believed in Jesus and experienced the richness of a diverse community united in him. The dividing walls of hostility melted away, and they aspired to live undivided.

Throughout the Bible, we see over and over again that the gospel brings people together who were once divided. We need this in our country, and it's exactly what the church can embody.

Let's be honest: racism has divided our society. Racism has divided the church. Where does this division come from? Race is a human construct, an elevation of distinctions in skin tone as a way to organize and separate people. It messes with our view of others, and of ourselves. Racism corrupts human societies and institutions. It also distorts the truth from Genesis that we are all image-bearers, created in the image of God.

The source of the problem runs deeper than this. Racism is also a spiritual problem. And spiritual problems require spiritual solutions. We aren't banking on human ingenuity to solve this intractable issue. We see the solution for racism and all its effects in the person of Jesus and the new humanity he calls us to. When we pursue becoming one new humanity, Jesus empowers us to remember and embody who we really are.

A New Kind of "New"

In these verses from Ephesians, Paul uses a unique word for *new*. The Greek language can be very specific. Often there are multiple Greek words that we consolidate into one word in the English language. Here Paul uses a specific word for *new*, and he does so on purpose. He could have used the word *neos*, which means chronologically new—simply the next thing to happen. Instead, Paul writes *kainos*, a word that suggests a new thing that has never been seen before in human history. It's a new kind of new.

Don't miss this important point! God has worked a miracle that's never been seen before! People who were ethnically diverse and therefore different and maybe even hostile toward one another are able to come together and be one new people. It's a bond deeper than ethnicity, a bond deeper than race, a bond rooted in Jesus. You are invited to be part of this miracle. UNDIVIDED invites us all to live out that miracle for racial solidarity, healing, and justice (all words we will define shortly) in our world.

This one new humanity is the animating vision that undergirds this book and our organization. The gospel is the good news that empowers us to live undivided. This is not a burden. This is not something we have to do. This is something we get to do—and we get to do it together.

A Flow of Racial Healing and Justice

When it comes to living undivided, at some point we all get stuck, which can lead to a dangerous state called stagnancy. Stagnant water has been trapped or undisturbed for a long time. Stagnant water creates the perfect environment for the growth of mold and other noxious substances that contaminate and destroy. Stagnant water attracts mosquitoes, which are associated with the spread of potentially deadly diseases like malaria, Zika fever, rotavirus, and more.

When it comes to race, our avoidance and passivity result in dangerous stagnancy in our congregations, neighborhoods, and nation. Every day we avoid confronting this evil, people are wounded. Some even die. The impact of a racially divided community gets in the way of every system and structure that surrounds us. Stagnant lives, stagnant communities, and stagnant churches drive the shared racial crisis we are now experiencing. Exploring this toxic stagnancy demands being confronted with some hard truths. Those tough realizations may look different depending on your race, point of view, and lived experiences.

As we work for racial healing and justice across the country, we often meet people who are ready to give up. Honestly, we sometimes find ourselves wrestling with despair. We also know the cost of losing hope and are reminded again and again that in the end these three remain: "faith, hope, and love" (1 Cor. 13:13).

Moses Maimonides, a Jewish philosopher and physician from the twelfth century, is credited with saying: "Hope is the belief in the plausibility of the possible rather than the necessity of the probable."[2] The author of Hebrews intertwines faith and hope: "Now faith is the assurance of things hoped for, the conviction of things not seen" (Heb. 11:1).

Hope is not easy, and it's a revolutionary act that often defies current conditions. Hope is also much more than wishful thinking. We have reasons to be hopeful.

Our hope rests first and foremost in God, who has faithfully acted in Scripture and throughout history by defying the necessity of the probable. God delivered the Hebrew people from bondage in Egypt, parted the Red Sea, gave David the hope and courage necessary to overcome Goliath, and yes, God raised Jesus from the dead!

We hope because God moved in history. God led faithful people to resist slavery, develop and lead the Underground Railroad, and fight for the abolition of slavery. We hope because God activated people to end apartheid in South Africa and an overthrow of colonialism throughout Africa, Asia, and the Americas. We hope because of the great cloud of witnesses who have gone before in the struggle for justice. As the Negro Spiritual says, "I'm so glad trouble don't last always."

We also hope because we are not alone. We're part of a growing UNDIVIDED community grounded in hope, and when one struggles, we lean on one another. Isolation leads to despair. True community keeps hope alive.

This book rests in hope, rooted in God, evident in history, made tangible through community.

A Word to Our Black, Indigenous, and People of Color (BIPOC) Siblings

We recognize that when we talk about race, it can often be traumatizing or even retraumatizing to our BIPOC siblings. We may share stories in this book that are triggering. There may be times when you need to put the book down, take a breath, and process what you're thinking or feeling. Please do so when necessary. We're grateful you're reading this book, as your voice and perspective are important in the journey toward living undivided. We also recognize that the sin of racism has infected us all, but in distinctly different ways. We invite you to examine where God wants to open your eyes and heart through what follows.

A Word to Our White Siblings

We know that engaging race as White people can be unsettling and even scary. We're reminded of what one White leader shared with us about how people can feel when wrestling with race: "You can't win, you CAN lose, and you can't quit." His honest reflection speaks to how fraught discussions of race can be for everyone involved. For our White siblings who are choosing to engage, thank you. Your voice, your story, and your unique perspective are so important for the redemptive and restorative path God desires to take us. Our encouragement to you is to approach this book with an open mind and an open heart. Listen to where God is getting your attention, then pause and reflect on what he's calling you to do to further the vision of one new humanity.

Stepping into the Flow with Hope

The UNDIVIDED vision, or what we call our North Star, is *a flow of racial healing and justice that repairs wounds and cultivates equitable systems where all people flourish.* In a world that continues to struggle with the evil of racism, we have hope for a better future. The language of flow appears throughout this book, and we contrast this with the state of spiritual or relational stagnancy. This language of flow is biblical and reveals the preferred future of a just world where all people will flourish.

We see this flow of hope in the vision the prophet Ezekiel describes in Ezekiel 47. He saw a vision of fresh water flowing from the temple of God in the city of Jerusalem. This fresh water, as it flows through the streets of Jerusalem, causes lush green trees to sprout up and grow. And of these trees, Ezekiel says, "Their fruit will be for food and their leaves for healing" (v. 12). Whose healing? What healing?

The answer is found in Revelation, where once again we see this flow of water from God's throne and these trees. But this time we get a clearer picture of the healing God has in store, when in Revelation 22:2, it says, "The leaves of the tree are for the healing of the nations." The nations! That means all of us! We're all invited to be healed in our relationships to God and one another.

Ezekiel's vision gets even better. As this fresh water flows through the desert and to the Dead Sea, where nothing grows, something even more miraculous happens: the fresh water from God's holy temple literally brings the Dead Sea to life! People fish on its banks and lush trees flourish in the middle of the desert. We believe that this flow, through the power of God, looks like a nourishing racial solidarity that heals the wounds of the past and cultivates a new, life-giving state of living undivided.

What Ezekiel imagined is not simply a restored temple, with an impact contained by the walls of the new structure. Ezekiel was able to imagine a community filled with healing and life, where all flourish. This is what the church could do today.

Why do we believe in this preferred future? A flow of racial healing and justice where all people flourish? Because according to the Bible, this isn't merely possible, it's inevitable. We also believe it because we see the firstfruits in the stories you'll read in this book. Honestly, these stories from our community help sustain our hope.

Tamika

Tamika is a Black woman who participated in one of our LivingUNDIVIDED cohorts, and her struggle to find an identity lost is representative of so many Black and Brown people in America.

Here's what Tamika says:

I was raised in North Carolina in a small, predominantly White, rural town. There, I was too Black. Then I moved to Baltimore when I was thirteen. There, I wasn't Black enough.

I moved into adulthood and entered the corporate world, where I still struggled to fit in. People would always say to me, "You talk so properly!" What they really meant was that I sounded *White*. At one point in my career, I changed my name to Tammy to fit an online persona I was trying to present in an attempt to claim some sort of an identity of my own.

To say I was having an identity crisis when I began the UNDIVIDED cohort would be an understatement. I didn't feel like I'd ever been accepted in any environment, and I wasn't even aware of all the pain I'd been in. But I decided to participate because I thought I might be able to contribute something to the conversation on racial justice in my city.

What I found was an environment that I could share in—and for the first time, feel comfortable sharing. What I didn't expect was the level of healing I would experience. God literally used the space of UNDIVIDED to heal me in areas I hadn't faced before. Now I'm on this journey to discover my own racial identity and how it impacts the woman I am today.

In fact, my UNDIVIDED experience inspired me to cut off all my hair! In an effort to conform to societal norms, I've done everything with my hair—from weaves to braids to relaxers. Looking back, I can see that I was chasing after whatever identity I could fit into. But I felt so free leaving UNDIVIDED, so confident and empowered, so unbound by all the expectations that had restricted me before, that cutting off my hair became my declaration of freedom.

Tamika's story is a microcosm of what's possible when we live undivided—what's already happening, in fact. Lives changed, identities found, healing experienced.

Carolyn

Carolyn is one of our LivingUNDIVIDED participants. Here's Carolyn's story:

When I think about my life before LivingUNDIVIDED, I was very passionate about racial reconciliation, and I was very passionate about learning more—about trying to help make things better in our city, because historically we've had a lot of racial unrest.

I did a lot of digging, trying to reeducate myself and expose myself to different voices. I would say I was very much on my own at that time. I was leading myself . . . trying to understand race, so I was very much limited.

After LivingUNDIVIDED, I had a community around me. Then, even more than that, I had a small group of people that grew into a large group of people in the justice team that was formed out of UNDIVIDED.

With that community around me, my perspective and my experience in regard to race and racial healing changed significantly. It changed from a solitary experience to a dynamic, fun, loving, challenging, bold experience. Those relationships are everything. They were the foundation of how we were able to change access to high-quality preschool in our city through Issue 44.

Those relationships are the foundation of how my family, which is now a multiracial family through adoption, can be healthy by having so many great perspectives and relationships with people of different cultural backgrounds. Those relationships are . . . my friends.

Before LivingUNDIVIDED, I was spending most of my time with people who had a similar cultural background to mine. Now I have a much more vibrant life experience. But even more than that, I feel like I have a pathway for how to make life more equitable in our city through the experiences I had with the LivingUNDIVIDED justice team and learning from different organizations like the AMOS Project. I was able to learn how to take some of those fundamental concepts from LivingUNDIVIDED and put them into action.

So much of that has to do with relationships. Before Living-UNDIVIDED, I had a strong desire to improve things in our city to bring healing and equity to our people, but I had no idea how to do it. I didn't know who I was supposed to do it with. And after, I feel like I made lifelong friends. I was able to explore a pathway through community organizing to help slowly build a more equitable city for my family, myself, my friends, and my neighbors.

LivingUNDIVIDED changed a lot in my life. I think of the experience as the springboard for a lot of big changes, a lot of healing—not just for myself, but for our entire community.

Solidarity, Healing, Justice

Any conversation about race in the twenty-first century is greatly helped by defining some key terms. We repeatedly use the following terms in the book and want to define them now.

Solidarity. We as human beings were made for humanity. Before sin entered the world in Genesis 3, God had already declared, "It is not good that the man should be alone" (Gen. 2:18). This invitation for solidarity, especially across differences, showed up in the early church when people from different languages "who believed were together and had all things in common" (Acts 2:44). In Acts 13, we see a multiethnic congregation of Jews and gentiles who were in solidarity together embodying the possibility and promise of community and a shared mission.

Solidarity is walking out our shared humanity and struggles together across race and ethnicity. We do not equate our contexts or experiences, but rather, through empathy and clarity regarding what is at stake for ourselves and those we love, we bind ourselves together not as allies but as kindred in Jesus.

34

Healing. Healing is the ongoing process of repairing wounds in ourselves, our relationships, and our communities. To heal, we must pause, reflect on the cause and nature of our wounds, and take the time that repair demands. While our contexts may look and feel different, all of us, regardless of race or ethnicity, have racial wounds that need healing. We invite God's spirit into the healing process, realizing a mix of honesty, courage, humility, confession, repentance, forgiveness, grace, and restitution may be required for healing.

Justice. Justice is action that cultivates equitable systems in which all people flourish. Justice must be active. Micah 6:8 calls us not to talk about justice, but to do justice. Racial justice in our context demands naming and addressing racial disparities baked directly into our institutions, systems, and culture. The Hebrew word for justice, *mishpat*, shows up over four hundred times in the Old Testament, and when Jesus launched his public ministry in Nazareth, he read from Isaiah 61, a text overflowing with the fruit of justice:

> The Spirit of the Lord is upon me,
>   because he has anointed me to bring good news to
>   the poor.
> He has sent me to proclaim release to the captives
>   and recovery of sight to the blind, to set free those
>   who are oppressed,
> to proclaim the year of the Lord's favor. (Luke 4:18–19)

After reading these words, Jesus told the congregation: "Today this scripture has been fulfilled in your hearing" (v. 21). Justice is part of the DNA of the Good News of Jesus. I once heard a well-respected preacher say that justice is the grand symptom of a life of faith. Cornel West puts it this way: "Justice is what love looks like in public."[3]

The UNDIVIDED Circle

This book will help you understand God's heart for racial healing, solidarity, and justice and give you a taste of what living undivided can look like in your own life through a process called the UNDIVIDED Circle. The process is ongoing. The steps of the UNDIVIDED Circle are ones we hope you choose to take over and over again. They're part of a cycle that must always be flowing through our lives and communities each day.

On this journey together, we will move around the circle and begin by exploring our *Roots*, our stories that make us who we are and bring us to this shared work together. We will then move to *Realize*, where we explore our history as well as the nature and persistence of racial disparities in our nation.

Next, we will invite you to *Respond*, and to do so in the context of community, and then to *Reckon* as we ground our identity in Jesus as one new humanity.

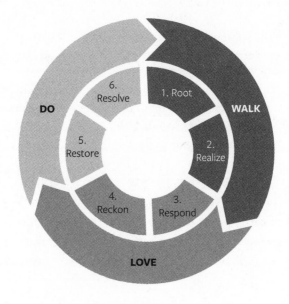

Finally, we will move into action as we share the call to **Restore** what is broken in God's world and our relationships and focus on the **Resolve** and courage necessary for us to collectively live undivided.

We want to let you know up front that we have a plan and a strategy crafted through experience. We've seen transformation that gives us hope for what God can do in and through you and your people. We're asking you to link arms with us as kindred in God's family, and with God to *walk* toward a better tomorrow by learning to *love* courageously by *do*ing what is good.

As Dave Ferguson writes in the foreword, our understanding of the gospel is that Jesus is King, Jesus has a kingdom, and Jesus's kingdom doesn't just look like us or like someone else—it looks like a diverse group of people all coming together, worshiping. In fact, that's exactly what's described in Revelation 7:9:

> After this I looked, and there was a great multitude that no one could count, from every nation, from all tribes and peoples and languages, standing before the throne and before the Lamb, robed in white, with palm branches in their hands.

The UNDIVIDED movement draws us closer to God's dream.

Because of the work of Jesus, racial unity isn't only possible, it's inevitable. At the end of time, when Jesus comes and reigns on the throne, there will be a reconciled people who are racially different but united through Christ's blood. Why not experience this right now?

Let's start living undivided!

EXAMINE YOUR STORY

1. Are you currently in a state of stagnancy or flow when it comes to the work of racial healing and justice?

2. If you're stagnant, what would it take to move you into a state of flow?

3. What do you hope to learn or gain from reading this book? Are you willing to release preconceived notions and perhaps even a little bit of pride to get there?

PART 1

ROOT

WALK HUMBLY

1. **ROOT**—Examining how our identity and journey prepare us for racial healing and justice.

2. REALIZE

What Is Good?

Back in the 1970s, drinking milk with meals must have been part of the parental instruction manual. Every lunch and dinner, I (Troy) had to drink a glass of milk with my meal. One problem—I hated milk.

When I was five years old, I had an epiphany. My dad was at work, so my mom was outnumbered by me and my two siblings (my brother and sister are twins and less than two years younger than I am). As my mom tended to my younger brother and sister, I made a bold decision. I scampered from my seat at the dining room table, hustled toward the kitchen sink, and boldly poured my milk down the drain.

I made it back, empty milk glass in hand. My mom was impressed by my milk-drinking skills! This was an exciting moment for me. I now had a tried-and-true strategy to handle the daily grind of drinking milk. Risky? Yes. Worth it? Absolutely.

As I began to plot future milk-pouring exploits, my mom went to the kitchen and happened to glance in the sink. And what did she see? Milk residue around the drain. Then came the question: "Troy Thomas, did you pour your milk down the sink?" The middle name said it all—I was in major trouble. My mom marched me into the kitchen, boosted me up, and asked me to explain how the milk got there.

I then realized the fatal flaw in my plan.

Three things immediately happened: I got a full glass of milk that I had to drink in full view of my mother, I grieved the loss of my inspired plan to permanently avoid milk, and I heard the terrifying words, "Wait until your father gets home."

When we're young, it's easy to sense what's good and what's not good. Lying about drinking our requisite glass of milk? *Not good.* But as we get older, those lines become blurry. What's good and what's not good isn't nearly as obvious as it was when we were five years old.

One of the banner verses in the UNDIVIDED community is Micah 6:8:

> He has shown you, O mortal, what is good.
>> And what does the LORD require of you?
> To act justly and to love mercy
>> and to walk humbly with your God. (NIV)

It's human nature to want to know the boundaries between good and bad. Perhaps it's not as much of a guessing game as we've made it—especially as followers of Jesus.

When it comes to race in America, what does it look like to embody what is good? What does this require of us individually and collectively? Thankfully, Micah breaks it down for us:

Do justice.

Love mercy.

Walk humbly.

Over the centuries, God has not changed—and neither have the truth and value of this charge. When it comes to race in our country, the words of Micah 6:8 make plain our path.

Judgment and Hope

The prophet Micah came onto the scene during a time of unrest and tension. Both Israel and Judah, the two nations that emerged following the reigns of Kings David and Solomon, were on the verge of collapse. Assyria, the superpower of the day, threatened to conquer both kingdoms.

What is the reason for this threat? The people of Israel were unfaithful to God. Instead of doing what was good, they'd chosen to worship the gods and goddesses of the surrounding nations while their leaders perpetuated injustice, trampling on the rights of the poor, orphans, widows, and immigrants.

Micah was saying, "You don't get it. You *still* don't get it. God has told you what is right. God has told you what is good."

What about us? Chaos and upheaval are all around. Everyone with eyes can see the trouble we're in. The world is getting hotter, both literally and figuratively. Fires in the western US get more intense every year, while drought threatens water levels in reservoirs that millions of people count on for daily life. Meanwhile, we are becoming more polarized, and both our rhetoric and our actions are becoming more violent. At the core of this division is racial tension and injustice.

It's at this present moment that Micah's words should echo in the heart of every follower of Jesus. What does it look like to represent Jesus well at this moment, when racism is ripping us apart? How should the church operate in such a polarized time?

To really understand and apply the message of Micah 6:8 to our lives and communities, it may help to take the verse in reverse order—because they really are layers of the same journey.

Out of the three "do good" actions listed in Micah, we will start with *walk humbly*.

Living the Circle

Nehemiah's story serves as an archetype of what it means to act for the sake of justice with a group of marginalized people, and Nehemiah's story begins with walking humbly.

We're drawn to Nehemiah because his story is deeply rooted in place, and we believe that must be true for living undivided in our day. The national problem can be too big, too overwhelming, or even too abstract. But when you root this work in place, like we've done in Cincinnati, you can make progress. This progress can extend beyond the place where you begin.

In the first chapter of his story, Nehemiah was in the capital city of Susa working as cupbearer to the king when his brother Hanani visited him from Judah. As cupbearer, Nehemiah was charged with tasting any wine brought to the king in case it was poisoned. This may sound like a job you would certainly *not* have wanted, but in reality, it came with a great deal of power. Think about it—when Nehemiah handed the king a goblet, the king trusted that whatever was inside was safe to drink. The level of faith the king had in his cupbearer was a matter of life and death.

Because of the king's trust in him, Nehemiah had political influence he could wield over the Persian royal court. So his brother showed up in the capital city of Susa and Nehemiah did what?

> I asked them about the Jews who escaped, those who had survived the captivity, and about Jerusalem. (Neh. 1:2)

Nehemiah *asked*. Asking is at the heart of walking humbly. He asked about a displaced and disgraced group of men and women who were returning home after being held in captivity. Nehemiah didn't have to ask. He could've turned the conversation to himself. Surely he had some good court gossip or a point of pride to share—he was likely the king's most trusted aide. Nehemiah also could have just asked after his brother and immediate family. But no. Nehemiah's first question to his brother was, "How are the people doing?"

Our guess is that most of you would do something to help someone in need if you were asked to, right? But how many of us seek opportunities to come to the rescue of hurting people—the marginalized members of our society?

Nehemiah's brother and friends responded: "The remnant there in the province who escaped captivity are in great trouble and shame; the wall of Jerusalem is broken down, and its gates have been destroyed by fire" (v. 3).

At that moment, Nehemiah had a choice. He could either say, "Man, that's too bad. Somebody should do something to help those poor people." Or he could do what he did—Nehemiah stepped into the UNDIVIDED Circle by examining his roots.

Step One: Root

In her book *Fortune*, Lisa Sharon Harper writes, "We have been deeply shaped by the stories we've told ourselves about God.

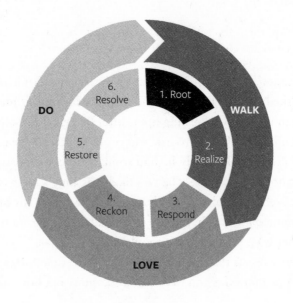

We have also been shaped by the stories we've told ourselves about ourselves."[1] This is the work of rooting—connecting to God and reconnecting with ourselves.

We joked about Nehemiah not offering court gossip or immediately turning the conversation with his brother toward himself. But Nehemiah's posture during this encounter with his brother is quite notable. Nehemiah's priority quickly became returning to his roots. He didn't just feel *for* the escaped captives, he felt *with* them.

This is what's required of anyone with a genuine desire to start the work of racial healing and justice. It must be a "we" and not a "they" approach. It must connect us to who we are in the deepest sense—children of God.

Aboriginal activist Lilla Watson is often credited with saying, "If you have come here to help me, you are wasting your time. But if you have come because your liberation is bound up with mine, then let us work together." This work begins by accepting the truth that racism hurts us all.

Nehemiah hurt because his people were hurting. Even though he was removed in location and status, he was still deeply connected to the pain of those he cared about—his brothers and sisters through the same heavenly Father. Nehemiah knew his roots, just as we must recognize ours.

Nehemiah knew he wouldn't be truly liberated until everyone was liberated. His liberation was bound up with the welfare of his brothers and sisters in Jerusalem. Because we are followers of Jesus, our liberation is bound up with our brothers and sisters of every racial and ethnic background.

Let's all start by examining our roots—our own stories. This requires us to ask ourselves tough questions, probing questions, about the journey that has brought us to this day and time and place. Unexamined stories, and unexamined lives, are stagnant breeding grounds for toxicity. The path of healing and justice must include rooting ourselves in our stories. Let's interrogate our personal experiences with racism so that we, too, can recognize just how bound together we are.

1 Chuck's Story

I was born in Philadelphia, Pennsylvania, in 1976. For the most part, for the first five years of my life, I was blissfully unaware of the concept of race. My entire life experience, with the exception of my White pediatrician and dentist and the Korean owners of the corner store in my neighborhood, consisted of interactions with Black people. Every authority figure in my life, from my schoolteachers to my spiritual leaders, was Black. While I couldn't have articulated this as a child, seeing people who looked like me in a range of professions and positions of influence gave me a lasting sense of pride in my racial identity.

Going to Church

This was especially highlighted on Sundays when my family attended Shekinah Revival Temple, a Black charismatic church led by my very own aunt Doris. The Black church wasn't only where I learned about the work of Jesus and all the heroes of the Bible, but it was also where I was introduced to the names and writings of Martin Luther King Jr., Booker T. Washington, and Frederick Douglass. I remember looking forward to our church's annual Black History Month program, which always featured a celebration of Black achievement in America.

When I reflect on my childhood, there was never a time when my faith in Jesus was separated from what it meant to live like him and to seek justice. It was never only about a personal relationship with Jesus. There was always a call to connect our following Jesus to the public and societal issues of the day. The preacher regularly applied the scriptural themes of unity and justice to Black experience at the time, all while "taking us to the cross" in every sermon—a hallmark of Black preaching.

While I experienced the best of Black culture at church, it was far from the only cultural influence. I remember the neighborhood block parties featuring home-cooked soul food and playing basketball on my street using milk crates with the bottoms cut out tied to telephone poles as our "hoops." The "Philly Sound" was on the rise, which meant long summer days defined by the soundtrack of Frankie Beverly & Maze, Teddy Pendergrass, and Patti LaBelle. I'm also firmly in the hip-hop generation, so my soundtrack also included Run-DMC, LL Cool J, and local rappers like Schoolly D, Cool C, and of course, DJ Jazzy Jeff & the Fresh Prince.

It was the era of break dancing too. The era of movies like *Krush Groove*, *Beat Street*, and *Breakin'* (I'm intentionally leaving out *Breakin' 2: Electric Boogaloo*). My friends and I would wait eagerly for someone to throw away a large cardboard box so we could convert it into our next break-dancing surface. We would flatten the box, turn on the boom box, and commence with headspins, poppin' and lockin', and our illest B-boy stance! However, try as I might, I was a terrible break-dancer. I was way too stiff! I was all lock and no pop!

I have so many fond memories of my childhood in Philadelphia. However, my neighborhood was a rough place at times. During the eighties' crack epidemic, I watched many of the people I had come to know and trust, including the parents of some of my friends and even two of my older siblings, battle drug addiction. I also saw it claim the lives of some of my friends who chose the path of selling drugs.

On the side of a home on the corner of the street where I lived, there's a mural dedicated to one of my friends who was murdered. Willie was a high-energy, tough-guy type. He had an explosive temper, and even though he wasn't very tall, he wasn't afraid to go toe-to-toe with anyone. Even though my personality was the polar opposite of Willie's, we were friends for years growing up in the neighborhood together.

In 1998, I was enjoying my freshman year at Duquesne University in Pittsburgh, when one night I got a call from my older brother, Rob. I could tell by the shakiness in his voice that the news wasn't good. He told me someone had killed Willie in a drive-by shooting. He was shot in front of the Korean-owned corner store where I'd spent many days hanging out with Willie and my friends, enjoying being kids. I don't quite know how to describe the experience of losing a childhood friend this way. I was deeply saddened. I also felt deep hopelessness, doubting whether my neighborhood would ever be a safe place again. I lost my friend. I also lost some of the innocence of my childhood.

Years later as I'm writing this, I live a firmly middle-class life. My kids attend private school, and most of my neighbors are White. Yet a part of me never forgets Willie and other friends and family members like him whose lives were snuffed out far too soon. No matter where I go and what I achieve, I remember where I have come from. It would be years later, when my world was expanded to include a more racially diverse set of friends and experiences, before I even had the language to consider my childhood through a racial lens. Overall, I'm grateful for my upbringing. Having undergone the range of Black experiences in America, I know the joy and tragedy of what it means to be Black.

Black businesses thrived in my neighborhood, and for a large portion of my childhood, nearly all the local political officials in office were Black, including the mayor. I also saw firsthand the debilitating impact of poverty, drugs, and broken families, and how when those factors are combined, families and communities alike erode into fragmented dysfunction (a phenomenon not unique to the Black community).

The "N" Word

I was fortunate to have a two-parent home. Ours was one of only two or three among the fifty-plus households on my street. My parents worked hard to provide me with a private-school education, which gave me access to further educational opportunities. I'm thankful I had these opportunities, but I remember how this often placed me in situations where I felt like I belonged to two very different, very separate, and, in so many ways, unequal Americas. If I had any notion of pretending this dichotomy didn't exist, two experiences from my childhood—one public and one personal—soundly eliminated any such hope.

My first school experience was at Second Macedonia Preschool, a small church-based school in my neighborhood. I had a great foundation there, which prepared me well for kindergarten. However, like so many other parents with kids in urban public schools today, my mom and dad did not want me to attend the neighborhood public school because it was underperforming and under resourced. Education was important to my parents. My father never graduated from high school, and my mother, who had a high school diploma, longed for her children to go further in their educational journeys. My parents enrolled me in Faith Christian School, which was a twenty-five-minute bus ride from my house. I had to walk to the public school to catch my bus to the northern suburbs where Faith Christian was located.

Faith Christian provided me with incredible learning opportunities, including smaller classes and unique experiences that, sadly, I never would have received at the neighborhood school. One of those experiences was visiting a working farm. It was the first time I had been on a farm. I got to ride a horse named "Paint" and shoot .22 rifles and bows and arrows. Not surprisingly, the school was mostly White. I went there from kindergarten through eighth grade, and for most of those years, I was one of only a handful of non-White children at the school.

Faith Christian was also the first place someone yelled "you n——r!" to my face. Yes, at the private Christian school my parents made sacrifices for me to attend. When the words came out of that person's mouth, it was a gut punch. You must realize that I loved my school, and I loved my friends. Being one of only a handful of Black kids hadn't been an issue up to this point. In fact, I loved that my friends had different backgrounds than I did. Faith Christian School was a safe place for me. But the experience of having someone call you such a degrading term felt anything but safe.

It happened when I was about nine years old. I'd always done well in school, and back in those days, I also did well as an athlete. I could play any sport, and most of all, I was fast. Whether it was football, track, soccer, or basketball, speed was my friend. I also had another friend, and to protect his identity, we'll call him Steve even though his real name is Michael (just kidding!). Steve was a competitive kid, and he'd get frustrated when he lost to me in anything. Really frustrated.

On one occasion, Steve got so angry that, in a fit of rage, he blurted out, "You n———r!" In case you hadn't guessed, Steve is White. It's impossible to describe what went through my preteen head when Steve's words landed on my ears. Suffice it to say that his epithet landed not only on my ears but also in my heart. Immediately, I felt less than, devalued, even violated. I can still remember the look of disgust on his face as he shouted at me. Even at that young age, I knew that word was well beneath the dignity and respect I deserved as someone created in God's image. I was so wounded by Steve's words that I was emotionally flooded, and I wanted to fight back—literally.

Steve's intention was to hurt me with the word, and it had its intended effect. But it also had an unintended consequence for Steve. A right hook to the jaw! After Steve called me other than my name, I almost instinctively took the hardest swing I could. Big mistake. See, while no one ever said calling someone the N-word wasn't acceptable at our nice little Christian school, punching other kids in the face was definitely a violation of the code of conduct. Both Steve and I were sent to the principal's office.

The principal asked me what happened, and when I told him, he was visibly shaken. I knew I deserved to be disciplined, and likely would be for what I'd done. There was also another reason to be a bit nervous about what the principal would do to me. Steve was his son.

Yeah. I never lead with that detail because it's always such a shocking twist. I punched the principal's kid right in the face.

There I was, thinking I might be suspended or even expelled from this good school that my parents had made sacrifices for me to attend and worked tirelessly to afford. I knew whatever pain I'd inflicted on Steve was about to be dealt back to me tenfold through whatever punishment my parents devised when I got home.

My principal sat across from me, looking both incredibly angry and deeply concerned. Then, in a surprising turn of events, he let me go. "Never, never let this happen again," he warned.

I felt an immediate rush of relief, thankful that I'd dodged a bullet. I promised myself I would never, ever put myself in that vulnerable position again. That promise lasted right up until the moment Steve called me the N-word again. Any guesses how I responded? If you guessed that I chose to be the bigger person and walk away, you'd be wrong.

What was the deal with me and Steve? Why was this word, even at that young age, able to be weaponized in the relationship between elementary-aged boys on a school playground? Now, to be clear, I'm fairly certain my principal was not attending KKK rallies on weekends, and I sensed genuine remorse on his face when he learned what his son had called me. I am not saying Steve learned that word at home, because I don't know that to be true. I do know that our families and upbringings shape our view on race in powerful ways. I know this because I have examined my response to Steve and in hindsight can see how my reaction to being called the N-word was shaped, in part, by having witnessed how my parents, and especially my father, responded to experiences of racism.

You Can't Trust White People

My parents loved God and loved me, and I experienced this love throughout my childhood. My parents were also wounded by their own experiences of racism, especially my dad. Born in 1928 in Saint Louis, Missouri (a former slave state now considered part of the Midwest), he experienced Jim Crow firsthand. If you're not familiar with the term *Jim Crow*, it refers to the set of laws and norms that enforced racial segregation in the United States.

He knew firsthand the world of "colored" bathrooms, "colored" movie theaters, and segregated education, making nearly every experience of my father's life separate and unequal. Through the years of my father's military service and employment, discrimination was the norm. Unsurprisingly, when I came along in 1976, my dad's clear and consistent message to me was, "Chuck, you can't trust White people."

When you're a kid and your parents say things, you tend to believe they're true. We all have a story when it comes to race, and that story has led to some conscious and unconscious conclusions or biases about people who are different from us. As someone who has come to believe that all people are created in God's image, I've found my roots, in part, by coming to grips with the ways my story around race competed with this spiritual truth.

Feelings Too Complex for Words

There's something else that shaped my view of race—one of those events that you never forget. On May 13, 1985, an event occurred that's still seared into my memory because of my dad's response. On that day, the city of Philadelphia dropped a bomb on a row house occupied by members of a Black radical religious organization called MOVE.

In preparing to tell this story in our book, I recently listed to the audio production *The Summer of '85*, narrated by Philadelphia native Kevin Hart. The production weaves together two things that happened in my hometown during the summer of 1985—the decision of then-mayor Wilson Goode to bomb the headquarters of MOVE and the July 13 Live Aid concert, where international rock stars gathered to raise money for the victims of the Ethiopian famine. *The Summer of '85* brought me again into the complexity of how race plays out in society.

First, let me tell you a bit more about MOVE. The MOVE organization had an anti-government, anti-technology, and anti-corporation philosophy. It was founded by Vincent Leaphart, a Black Philadelphia native who later changed his name to John Africa out of reverence for the African continent. MOVE was founded in 1972 and combined Black revolutionary ideas with a back-to-nature and pro-environmental view of the world. Long before such things were broadly popular, the group was into composting, homeschooling, and eating a raw-food diet. They also spoke out against war and police brutality.

MOVE engaged publicly through highly disruptive but non-violent protests in public places like the Philadelphia Zoo. Many residents found their lifestyle to be a nuisance, and they caught the eye and ire of the city government on several occasions.

Philadelphia had recently elected its first ever Black mayor, W. Wilson Goode. Goode had run his campaign on being a candidate of the people and addressing the ongoing corruption and aggressive policing that marked the Philly police department at the time. He was also asked repeatedly by the neighbors of MOVE to do something about the group, which was moving from nuisance to genuine threat. Rather than getting better, the situation continued to worsen, and eventually escalated into the fateful events of May 13, 1985.

Mayor Goode gave the order to evict the MOVE organization from its residence. What began as an eviction by the city devolved into a bombing that left not only the residents of Osage Avenue but also many residents of Philadelphia, especially Black people, asking how a city could justify that kind of violence against its own citizens.

It was later reported that the police fired over ten thousand rounds of ammunition in under ninety minutes at the MOVE row house, which also housed children. Firefighters were on the scene throughout the day, but the police and fire departments decided to let the fire burn to force the occupants from their houses.

While I remember the incident, I was only nine years old at the time, so there was no way I could have understood the complexity of the situation. But what I do remember clearly is the look on my dad's face as the news covered the fire and standoff live on local TV. I remember my dad letting out a deep sigh and fighting back tears. I now understand that in that moment, my dad was experiencing the often confusing and conflicting emotions associated with racial events.

The sight of a city government firebombing Black people felt unimaginable in 1985. Perhaps as he watched this unfolding, he was reminded of the state-sanctioned violence against Blacks during the Civil Rights era. I just know I will never forget the look of familiar sadness in his eyes. What thoughts and feelings does this story evoke in me today? What does it evoke in you as you read this? So many situations like this seem to evoke feelings too complex for words.

Central High School

One of the places I experienced the joy of a diverse environment was my high school. After eighth grade, I attended a large public school called Central High School—a large, diverse college preparatory school in the heart of the city. My high school sat on top of a grassy hill and had four entrances called the four "lawns." Every lawn had its own clique or type of kids who hung out there. The south lawn was for the rock 'n' roll crowd, the east lawn was for the jocks, the west lawn a potpourri, and the north lawn was where all the Black kids hung out. Each lawn drew a set of students who shared the same story, the same view of the world.

You can think of the lawns at my high school as a metaphor for the challenge of not just coexisting as different racial groups but coming together and experiencing solidarity and relationship. Even in a place like Central High School, where there was a tremendous opportunity to build relationships across racial lines, many kids chose to retreat to the lawn that most represented who they were and the story they already believed.

Central High School redefined my story on race in good ways. I chose to engage with students across the lawns and had friends of many hues and backgrounds. One of these relationships was with my friend Quentin, who was also known as Little Bear. Quentin was a big guy, one of the leaders on the football team, and of Indigenous ancestry. He and I had many great conversations about his background and culture, and we were able to connect over a common love of hip-hop music. As a result of relationships like the one I had with Quentin, my perception shifted. Many of the stereotypes I once held lost their foothold in my belief system.

The rich and diverse tapestry of friendships I had in high school remains part of my fondest memories and my most powerful lessons. Those friendships have motivated me to always seek out, invest in, and enjoy relationships across the lawns of life, race, and society. In fact, that desire is the reason that, after college when I moved to Cincinnati, I started attending Crossroads Church, where I'm now a pastor.

Finding My Way to Crossroads

Five years before I moved to Cincinnati, a group of eleven people started a church there called Crossroads. The heart of the church was to be a place for people who had given up on church but hadn't given up on God. This meant stripping away a lot of the rituals that churches do out of habit and reimagining the experience through the eyes of a new person who needs a place to wrestle with the truth of Jesus in language that resonates with them. Even though I grew up in the church, as I approached my midtwenties, that's exactly what I needed.

I had always been a church attender and had a relationship with God from an early age. Yet through my college years and into the beginning of my corporate career, many of the traditions of the churches I attended had grown stale and meaningless in my mind. Crossroads was a fresh approach to the "old-time religion" I was raised on. It was also 99 percent White.

I was new to Cincinnati when I first attended Crossroads, and I loved everything about it except its lack of diversity at the time. I was twenty-four, single, and in a brand-new city. I thought, *While I like this church, if I go here, it's possible I won't have a single Black friend in Cincinnati.* So even though I liked Crossroads, I decided to join a predominantly Black church on the other side of town. The Black church was very familiar to me, and it felt like coming home. I also began to meet people who looked like me.

I was good with my decision until one day I wasn't. It's not like I had a negative experience at the church or wasn't growing spiritually. I can only describe it as one of the times in my life when God's direction to me was so clear, I *almost* heard him say it in an audible voice: *go back to Crossroads.*

Desiring to follow God in obedience, I left the Black church. Almost immediately I was invited to join a small group of men for a weekly Bible study at Crossroads. Though I was the only Person of Color, I quickly developed a deep brotherhood with the men in that circle. We did life together, from eating meals to watching games to everything in between. In this group, I had some of the most honest conversations with White men about race that I'd ever had in my life. While the discussions weren't always easy, they were the seeds of what would later become the UNDIVIDED movement. I've now been part of the Crossroads community for over twenty years, and it continues to be a spiritual home where I experience the richness that comes from being in community with people who, while from different backgrounds, pursue unity and common cause through our shared allegiance to Jesus.

2001 Unrest

While Crossroads was and continues to be my spiritual home, my experience there has included many moments of challenge. Early on, I experienced this tension as everyone in Cincinnati processed the killing of nineteen-year-old Timothy Thomas by a city police officer. This officer-involved shooting exposed the fault lines of racism and mistrust that have often defined the Black community's relationship with law enforcement in this nation. As you might have guessed, it also brought back personal memories from my childhood of the police response to the MOVE organization in Philadelphia.

In the wake of the Timothy Thomas shooting, Cincinnati erupted in unrest, leading to a curfew and lockdown on the city. The leadership at Crossroads had called for a gathering early that evening to pray for peace and unity. Although I was fairly new to Crossroads at the time, I decided to attend.

It was rattling to see my city in that kind of unrest—the kind that I'd only ever seen in black-and-white images from the 1960s. As a twenty-five-year-old, I related to the expressions of fear and anger echoing in the streets. I really needed encouragement and felt it would be good to be around fellow Christ followers. I arrived and, not surprisingly, was one of very few non-White people there. While this was common for me not only at church but also at work, on this day I felt wary and weary because I had only a majority-White environment in which to process my pain.

The prayer gathering began and quickly turned into an "open mic" opportunity for people to pray out loud. It was great to be in that room, surrounded by others who shared a desire for more of God's presence and peace in this painful and divisive situation. Then it happened. I don't know who the person was, but someone began to pray a very accusatory prayer.

I remember them praying that "those people" would, in essence, get their acts together, shut up, and move on. They never said "those Black people," but trust me when I tell you that they didn't have to. I remember opening my eyes to try to identify who was praying, but in a room of a couple hundred people, I never figured out who it was. After this person finished praying, the meeting continued. But I was so angry, I couldn't hear anything else after that.

For me, this was a "crossroads" moment, and one of many I've had in my two decades at the church. I recognized that I had a choice: I could leave Crossroads and find a church where I didn't have to run the risk of being offended in a prayer meeting, or (and I'm so glad I chose this option) I could recognize that no church is perfect, and in fact, any church wanting to reflect more of the diversity of God's kingdom would choose to embrace and not avoid the inherent racial tension in America.

David Bailey, a friend of ours and the founder of Arrabon, an organization that works for racial solidarity, once told me something I try to always remember: "The presence of diversity in a church doesn't guarantee unity. The only thing it guarantees is conflict." David's work, like ours, leads churches in how to create a reconciling culture instead of just letting the conflict go unaddressed or unresolved.

Little did I know that the choice to stay and engage at Crossroads would lead to me ultimately leaving a great corporate job to answer a new call to be a pastor there.

Brave Journey

Fast-forward to May 2015. I had been a pastor at Crossroads for eight years. One of the rhythms there is to do an annual teaching series we call the journey. We focus on a specific topic together, and everyone does personal work and gets into small groups to go on a journey of learning and discovery concerning that specific topic. The season is a highlight of our ministry calendar, and it always leads to incredible spiritual breakthroughs. In 2015, our theme was the "Brave Journey." Everyone selected a goal they felt challenged by God to accomplish. I thought mine would be something like being a better husband or completing a triathlon.

Well, I was wrong. I spent some time praying and reading the Bible in week two of the journey and had a moment when everything got *real*. The years 2014 to 2015 were yet another period of pain in not just the Black experience but in the American experience with racism. There are too many stories to tell them all here, such as seventeen-year-old Trayvon Martin's death at the hands of George Zimmerman or the twelve-year-old child from Ohio, Tamir Rice, whom officers shot and killed after mistaking his toy gun for the real thing or the murder of five Dallas police officers in the wake of the racial tensions that gripped our country in 2016.

Do you remember those days? Try to remember how you were processing our nation's racial tensions bubbling to the surface. What was the story you believed about what was happening back then? Was it the story of a systemic problem rooted in racial inequality? Was it the story of why police can't be trusted? Was it the story of how a few isolated and unfortunate events were being blown out of proportion?

Like you, I experienced a mix of pain, frustrations, and deep questions. I also heard a clear call to be a voice for racial solidarity and justice. This was to be my brave journey. I had no idea just what that meant, and I certainly didn't have any idea of how to accomplish it. So I did the only thing I knew to do—I told someone. Well, actually, I told about twenty thousand people a week later when I gave the first of many messages on God's call for the church to embrace racial healing, solidarity, and justice. At this time, Crossroads had grown to be about 80 percent White and 20 percent non-White. Our church, and especially the largest campus, was growing in ethnic and racial diversity. Still, as the Black pastor calling for racial solidarity, I wasn't sure how I'd be received. The response was overwhelmingly positive. People sent me emails (mostly the good kind), people (of various races and ethnicities) shared their own stories of pain around race, and above all, people said they wanted to do *something*.

Choosing a New Story

As I reflect on my life and calling, I continue to believe that a new story is possible in the church and in our country. I have committed my life to this good work. In Zechariah 9:12, God calls his people "prisoners of hope." I want to live my life as a prisoner of hope. As someone who both believes in and is working toward a world that is less divided tomorrow than we are today.

In recent years, TikTok and Twitter users have become familiar with the phrase "they understood the assignment." It's slang used to praise someone who is going above and beyond to do a good job. Through leading or experiencing UNDIVIDED, thousands of people in nearly one hundred cities across the country are understanding the assignment. They're finding their place in God's story of racial healing, solidarity, and justice. They're becoming prisoners of hope.

Here's some good news: we don't have to remain locked into a view of race based on the limited perspective of our story. Through relationships that bring us into proximity with people from different backgrounds, we get the tools we need to choose a new story. To be clear, this good work needs *you*, and it needs to be influenced by your story!

Racial healing is baked into the mission of the church. It's all throughout the Bible, from Genesis to Revelation. The story God is telling, the story that's growing like a mustard-seed movement, is about how God is reconciling the entire world to himself and is inviting everyone, everywhere, to join in.

An undivided church isn't just a pipe dream. It's an inevitable reality, and it's already happening. If you're willing to fight stagnancy and commit to flowing through the UNDIVIDED Circle, you can be part of it. You are meant to be part of it.

Your first step is already happening right now. As you read our stories and examine your own, we invite you to pay attention to how yours is rooted in the larger story of God.

2 Troy's Story

I do not remember my family talking much about race when I was a child growing up in Anderson, Indiana. My town had racial diversity, as our 22,000 General Motors jobs were a pull for White and Black families throughout the middle part of the twentieth century. While most of these families, like mine, were White, some Black families made their way to Anderson as part of what is known as the Great Migration. The Great Migration was an era when well over five million Black people headed north and west between roughly 1910 and 1970. The west side of Anderson was the Black part of town, but my family lived several miles north of the city in a nearly all-White subdivision.

My first real engagement with Black people came not through neighbors or school but through the other thing Anderson was known for: basketball. At the time, Anderson High School had the second-largest high school basketball gymnasium in the world, seating just shy of nine thousand people, and it would regularly sell out. In Anderson, high school basketball was such a big deal that my grandparents held season tickets (yes, to watch teenagers play basketball) into their late sixties.

Race and Basketball

When I was growing up, my father was a math teacher at North Side Middle School and also coached the eighth-grade basketball team. As a young boy, I tagged along to my dad's Saturday morning basketball practices and some of their games. His team consisted of thirteen- and fourteen-year-old boys, but from my four-year-old perspective, they might as well have been Michael Jordan, Larry Bird, and LeBron James.

My father's teams were typically around half White and half Black. My dad would occasionally give some of his players a ride home after a road game or practice. He would fill our old station wagon with five or six teenage guys, often all Black, and I'd sit shoved in somewhere with three team members in the back seat, having the time of my life. My first cross-racial experiences weren't filled with fear or anxiety or trauma; rather, they created indelible positive memories.

Growing up in the 1970s and 80s, I also saw portrayals of Black families and culture on television, particularly *The Jeffersons*, *Different Strokes*, and *Good Times*. These shows offered different glimpses of Black life at the time, with *Different Strokes* depicting a wealthy White family who adopted two Black children, *The Jeffersons* showing an upper-class Black family, and *Good Times* portraying a working-class Black family.

In sixth grade, we took our final elementary school field trip to Chicago to the Museum of Science and Industry. I remember having a fantastic time with friends that day, a twelve-year-old experiencing relative freedom from adult oversight in an awesome museum for hours on end! I also remember the drive into Chicago, which went through the south side of the city. With *Good Times'* Jimmie "JJ" Walker's constant references about "the ghetto" on my mind, I began looking for signs of the ghetto or housing projects along the interstate, things I had seen only on television. I enthusiastically shouted about my search for the ghetto during the bus ride, which included one Black classmate amid a sea of White faces. My good friend Michelle told me, "Troy, you are being inappropriate right now." She went on to say that my words were offensive to Black people.

I first became a little defensive. But mostly I remember feeling ashamed—and also really confused. I got quiet and turned inward for the remainder of the drive to the museum. I had said something inappropriate, and I didn't know how to process the experience. So I didn't talk about it with anyone. I buried it.

Looking back years later, I wonder if I didn't internalize the idea that race was a "hot potato" to be touched and engaged at one's own risk—a cause for fear or at the very least hesitancy. I felt like I had messed up, and if I had kept my mouth shut, the day would have gone much better.

Like that school bus ride, most of my other early childhood experiences were in nearly all-White enclaves. My church, Bethany Christian Church, averaged over five hundred attendees every Sunday, and none of them were Black. My elementary school had around six hundred students, and there were only two Black families in the entire school.

Once I got to middle and high school, there was a bit more diversity. Of the eight hundred or so students, about 5 percent were Black. Most of these students were part of our school due to bussing, a practice where Black students were transported to schools outside their typical district boundaries to increase diversity and enhance educational opportunities. At the time, I welcomed the small amount of diversity at school. I had some subconscious awareness that many of the Black students were in a difficult situation, entering a space where White people and culture were centered. If nothing else, I wanted to be a welcoming presence.

While I was in middle school, I felt a strong calling from God to be a pastor when I became an adult. At Rainbow Christian

Camp near the metropolis of Converse, Indiana (sorry, no connection to Chuck Taylors or the athletic apparel company), I attended a service that ended with the speaker asking those who were willing to commit their lives to Christian service to come to the front of the stage. While I was nervous to "go public" in this way, I walked to the front and said yes to the call. After this, being a Christian was part of my identity, and I was also tied up in being seen as the "good kid."

A few years ago, a major controversy emerged when photos went viral of the Virginia governor at the time wearing Blackface while in college. When that story hit, my mind immediately went back to another memory from that very same year at church camp when I made my commitment to become a pastor. This was the summer of 1983, and Michael Jackson's *Thriller* album was having a legendary run at the top of the music charts. I was a tall, awkward, skinny fourteen-year-old with little talent and less self-awareness.

When the camp announced talent night, I decided I was the person to demonstrate Michael Jackson's famous moonwalk while a boom box played "Billie Jean." For anyone who knows me, or has known me, the level of delusion that led me to think I could dance in front of a room of over a hundred teenagers is hard to overestimate. On the plus side, I guess it demonstrates some amount of courage? But in the days leading up to the performance, I wanted to get fully into character, so I thought about adding shoe polish to my face as a way to more fully embody and emulate Michael Jackson.

The dean of camp that year and a pastor at my home church learned of the idea and had a conversation with me, briefly explaining the very painful history and impact of blackface in the US. He helped me understand that blackface created caricatures of Black people that elevated negative stereotypes to entertain all-White audiences. David Ray made it clear in no uncertain terms that I wasn't to join this legacy on his watch.

I again became defensive and tried to rationalize my intent. After this conversation, I had some sense that what I had intended to do was wrong, but I didn't fully understand the "why." This story sticks in my memory, though, because it's from a time when I was beginning to understand how complex race is in this country. I knew about slavery. I knew a bit about separate water fountains and Martin Luther King Jr. I had heard snippets of King's famous speech from the March on Washington. But here it was more than a century after the end of slavery and fifteen years after Dr. King's assassination, and I was just learning that dealing with race was difficult and there were minefields I didn't understand and couldn't anticipate. Regretfully, I didn't research the issue further when I got home from camp. Oh, for the record, I did get on stage and wow my peers with my moon-walking. I am very grateful I was fourteen years old well before every teenager could video anything at a moment's notice!

In high school, I became friends with a Black female classmate who was in several advanced classes with me year after year. I vividly recall during my sophomore year talking to my friend and another Black student. Somehow interracial dating came up in the conversation. I told them that because I was going to be a pastor someday, I could only date or marry a White person. I had the impression (accurate or not) that my church and the churches I had been around would not accept an interracial couple, and this would somehow get in the way of sharing the good news of Jesus. As I said these words, I expected my caveat regarding my personal views and the sincerity of my devotion to God to be well received, even applauded.

But then I saw their responses on their faces—confusion, hurt, even disbelief. I knew my words had negatively impacted them, and a flood of emotions began to stir within me. The mix of pride and confidence that I had felt earlier in the conversation quickly shifted to uncertainty and regret. I knew I had wounded my classmates and wanted to undo the entire conversation. What I saw as an example of devotion, they interpreted as racial discrimination and a subtle, or not-so-subtle, implication that to be Black was a problem.

I liked the perception of being a part of cross-racial connections and wanted the benefits of having friends who were different from me, but only up to a point. I didn't want to pay the price of truly examining my theology, behavior, beliefs, or sense of self. I wanted to be a hero and play it safe at the same time. I realized in the moment that I had failed my friends, and while I defended my choice with a gospel veneer, I had a subtle suspicion that I was maybe, perhaps, simply wrong.

Growing Passion for Racial Justice

After high school, I attended Franklin College in Indiana, where I studied religion and philosophy. My religion professor assigned *The Autobiography of Malcolm X*, a book that reshaped my fairly limited knowledge of this significant Black civil rights leader and offered a first-person story that helped me make some sense of my cross-racial experiences.

I made new connections, recognizing how the experiences I had as a White guy from the Midwest suburbs differed from Black experiences. We have similarities and very real differences, and I recognized these distinct contexts affected not only my preferences but also my opportunities and even my relationship with Jesus.

I then went to Princeton Theological Seminary between 1991 and 1994, which is where my concern for racial solidarity and justice moved from a head issue to a heart and gut calling. Having had my interest piqued by my exposure to Malcolm X, I took a course on the theology of James Cone my first year. Cone was a leading voice of the Black theology movement for fifty years, working to understand God, Jesus, and Scripture through the lens of the Black American experience. He was a professor at Union Theological Seminary in New York City and penned several important books, including *The Cross and the Lynching Tree* and *The Spirituals and the Blues*. I read James Cone's first book, *Black Theology and Black Power*, during college. This book helped launch Black theology in the late 1960s. Cone argued that his view of God and relationship with Jesus did not have to come through the gaze and words of the White theological establishment.

During the course at Princeton, we read several more of Cone's books and watched an episode each week of the PBS documentary series *Eyes on the Prize*. The first episode includes the story of Emmett Till, a fourteen-year-old from Chicago, whom Carolyn Bryant, a White woman working at a local store, falsely accused of whistling at her or saying "Bye, baby" as he left a store in Money, Mississippi, in 1955.

Roy Bryant and J. W. Milam, two of Carolyn Bryant's White relatives, murdered Till a few days later for breaking racial taboos. Although they were clearly guilty and confessed their crime to a reporter with *Look* magazine several weeks later, the all-White jury listened to the defense attorney's challenge in his closing argument: "Your fathers will turn over in their graves if [Milam and Bryant are found guilty], and I'm sure that every last Anglo-Saxon one of you has the courage to free these men."[1] After deliberating for about an hour, the jury pronounced a not-guilty verdict. Following their acquittal, Bryant and Milam expressed to reporters how glad they were and then kissed their wives. I remember sitting in that college classroom, horrified. In my guilt and shame at that moment, I looked at my hands and wished they were a different color.

When I heard the story of Emmett Till in 1992, I heard a story I'd never known before. I also saw a side of this country I didn't fully understand. I remember feeling a bunch of emotions in that moment and in the coming days. I felt ashamed that people who looked like me had murdered this young boy and others who looked like me had let them get away with it. I felt angry, wondering why this story, and others like it, had not found their way into any of my history classes growing up. I felt sad. I also felt a little defensive. While I could blame gaps in my history classes growing up or the books I'd read, I had also chosen not to think too deeply about what lynching actually looked like and hadn't explored my feelings about the human toll it took on lives and families. The tragedy of Emmett Till moved me to engage race at a deeper, more emotionally honest level.

Recently, I was on an early morning flight from New York City to Chicago, and seated next to me was a Black man who looked to be in his early seventies. I looked over as he shuffled through the movie selections before settling on *Till*, the 2022 movie about Emmett Till's murder and its impact on his family and the nation. While I tried to focus on other work during the flight, on multiple occasions I heard and sensed my seat mate choking back tears. I was reminded yet again of the pain and trauma that racism and racial violence has seared into all our psyches, and particularly in the hearts of my BIPOC friends.

When I first began to feel the impact of racism, I'm grateful that I didn't remain alone as I sorted out my feelings and struggles. Looking back, I would recall this moment as an example of God's kindness. Paul writes in Romans 2:4, "Do you not realize that God's kindness is meant to lead you to repentance?" I remember several lengthy late-night conversations with Wilmot Allen, a Black seminary student from Cincinnati who lived down the hall from me. I shared my confusion, lament, anger, and frustration and began to process my sense of guilt and shame. I also listened a lot. My friend embodied a beautiful blend of patience, challenge, grace, and love that turned a season of deep realization into a catalyst for the Holy Spirit to reshape me.

In retrospect, I went through a process that Chuck often cites from 2 Corinthians 7:10: "For godly grief produces a repentance that leads to salvation and brings no regret, but worldly grief produces death." I went through a several-months-long process of godly grief in part because I didn't go through it alone. I had a foretaste of what it's like to live undivided, thanks to my friend Wilmot.

Time to Act

A few months later, in the spring of 1992, a jury reached a verdict in the trial of four Los Angeles police officers who had kicked and beaten an unarmed Black man named Rodney King as he lay prone on the side of the road. A Los Angeles resident videoed the beating. Honestly, I knew a little about the case but was not following the trial closely. I was preparing for final exams and my wedding day, which was about a month away. But I certainly remember the verdict.

A grand jury indicted the officers, but the judge changed the site of the trial to a neighboring county, and no Blacks were on the jury. They found the LAPD officers not guilty, and soon after, South Central Los Angeles erupted in violence.

In response to the unrest in Los Angeles, the administration of Princeton Theological Seminary called a forum at the school chapel to reflect, pray, and consider possible action. After I arrived and found a seat that evening, I looked around and quickly realized that White students were in the minority. Of the 800-plus students at Princeton, there were about 40 Black students, and I saw nearly all of them in the chapel. There were about 150 Korean and Korean American students, and around 50 showed up. I learned during the forum that evening that many Korean-owned businesses had been affected by the unrest in LA. I was one of only a dozen of the 600 White students on campus who showed up.

I don't remember a lot of what was said that evening, but I recall the feelings I sensed in the room. Professors and faculty who had lived through the Civil Rights Movement were lamenting the lack of progress toward racial justice. Many students were angry about the verdict, and we debated how best to advance the cause of racial justice in our nation and the church. Meanwhile, several of the Korean and Korean American students knew that Korean-owned businesses had suffered the brunt of the unrest. The cost to their community was palpable, and they expressed a mixture of frustration, grief, and anger, feeling caught between wanting justice for Rodney King and their concern for their own communities. As I processed all these reactions, a strong sense of resolve welled up in my spirit; I felt I could no longer be content with conversations and ruminations on race in this country. It was time to act.

I had reasons not to get involved. My family hadn't been directly affected. The pain revealed during that chapel meeting, and evident in Los Angeles, didn't seem to directly impact my life. Also, we were getting ready for final exams and papers, so I had plenty of academic work on my plate. And finally, my wedding to my wife, Amanda, was just a few weeks away. Suffice it to say, I could've sat this one out. But I also sensed that if I waited to act this time, I may never get engaged. I learned that for me, waiting to respond results in me being tentative, cautious, and passive. I become stagnant.

I stuck around after the forum that evening and got involved in additional meetings, conversations led by Black students about what to do next. When a few of the students decided to form a new campus organization called Seminarians for Justice (look, I'm not saying we were wordsmiths, but we were passionate!), I signed up and attended the first meeting the next day.

That was my first experience advocating for racial justice. My fellow Black students shared stories about being followed and surveilled while they shopped in downtown Princeton, New Jersey, so we started a campaign to end this practice. We pushed for greater racial equity on our campus. We also decided to head to Washington, DC, for the "Save Our Cities, Save Our Children" march—a rally led by mayors of major cities around the nation. I got up very early to board a school bus for an all-day trip to the nation's capital, where we joined over thirty-five thousand people calling for justice for Rodney King and for our nation to address the underlying despair affecting children and families in our cities.

I imagined how my life could be a response to the clear voice of God and the often-unheard voices of BIPOC friends experiencing injustice. This ragtag group of seminarians continued to meet throughout the next school year, and I learned from and acted as part of a multiracial effort for justice.

One of my first lessons from my Black classmates was that I did not have all the answers, and I was not the expert. I'd been near the top of my class all through high school and college and had a great GPA at seminary. Part of my identity was my ability to pontificate on the topic at hand, often believing I was the smartest guy in the room. On this team, however, I quickly realized my arrogance would not serve me or anybody well. My colleagues listened patiently to my attempts to shape our direction, and while I felt included, this was not a group that needed or wanted my leadership.

To be honest, my typical reaction to this type of environment was to disengage. I don't like being in spaces where I feel unsure and ill-equipped. I sometimes wondered if this team, and even this work, was for me. At the same time, I felt included and appreciated—not for my leadership but for my resolve, my growing ability to listen, and my commitment. They also gave me a sharper vision for my call: to learn, to be faithful, and to act as part of a multiracial community to prepare myself for future assignments for racial justice.

The Work of Repentance

Following seminary, Amanda and I moved to Cincinnati, where I served as a pastor for nearly nineteen years at University Christian Church. Partly because of my experiences with Seminarians for Justice and partly because it was somewhere we found a house we could afford, we chose to live in a largely Black neighborhood. We were the only White family on the block. I felt like this decision was a mark of faithfulness at the time, a clear demonstration of our family's commitment to racial reconciliation. We also felt welcomed by the other residents on the block. As I walked our dog every day, I had conversations with neighbors about everything from the weather to our local sports teams and enjoyed younger children eagerly coming over to pet our dog.

Amanda and I lived in this home for over a decade, and everyone would check on each other. Our next-door neighbors, who were about ten years older than us, looked after us. One Saturday they knocked on our door to kindly let us know our car had rolled into the street. This was one of those embarrassing incidents that they may still be laughing about decades later. So how did my car end up in the middle of the road? We had recently bought a "state of the art" Geo Metro with manual transmission, and our little driveway was on a small incline. I had absentmindedly failed to engage the parking brake when arriving home, and the rest is history. I sheepishly rushed out to return our car to the driveway, triple checking that I had successfully engaged the parking brake! On normal days and embarrassing days, this community felt like home.

As a young pastor, I sought relationships in town with other clergy for support and encouragement and to challenge me. Over the years, a diverse cadre of pastors emerged. We prayed for each other and shared our lives with one another. One of the pastors I met was Ray McMillan, the passionate and fearless Black leader of Faith Christian Center. He also founded Race to Unity, an organization committed to building bridges across race through relationships. Ray challenged us to take an honest look at our many Founding Fathers who were complicit with slavery.

Pastor McMillan began leading regular monthly meetings with a group of pastors to address our country's racist heritage. Many of us, including evangelicals, celebrate George Washington, Thomas Jefferson, and other Founding Fathers as nearly flawless heroes. This was part of my upbringing. My public school history courses venerated these figures, and I respect them for their vision, courage, and leadership. I learned that for Ray and other Black pastors in the group, these founders' compromises over slavery, decisions to enslave people, and racism disqualified them from Christian hero status.

Because of Pastor McMillan's passion and persistence and some strategic pressure placed on a major evangelical leader through letters and intermediaries, a group of us secured an in-person sit-down in one of the epicenters of evangelicalism. We had a nearly five-hour meeting on racism and the dangers of hero worship of our nation's Founding Fathers. Those around the table included the founder and president of a huge international Christian organization, a former presidential candidate, and the former president of a national evangelical group.

I believed we should be able to admire people while also fully reckoning with their flaws and sinfulness. Take, for example, a celebrated hero like King David. When we read 1 and 2 Samuel, we get a glimpse of King David at his best and his worst. Likewise, I felt we could celebrate the American founders while also having a full understanding of their triumphs and failures. This is a crucial part of the gospel—that we all fail, and through God's grace, we can fail forward. God is looking not for perfection but for "a broken spirit . . . and contrite heart" (Ps. 51:17).

After a grueling meeting, we made little progress. I had moments of anger, frustration, and weariness as the time ticked by. One of the "biggest" names at the table said that even if what we were saying about our founders was true, "I can't take this story away from our kids." I was dumbfounded. "This story" was a false narrative of our nation's history that left out the complicated messiness and racism of many of its Founding Fathers. I wondered why this powerful White evangelical leader elected to preserve a myth rather than wrestle with the truth. I recognized how hard it can be for me to publicly change, particularly when my identity and reputation are tied up with a position that I now questioned. I knew that change without cost was usually easy, but when change demanded a lot of me,

I was tempted to dig into the status quo. I wondered if this was what was going on with this leader.

After that meeting, I returned to Cincinnati convinced I had the best strategy for moving forward from this harrowing experience. We wanted to continue to push those we met to see the truth, but we debated about the best way forward. Although I had learned a few things in seminary about being in a multiracial organization, I still had a bias that, as a White male, I knew the best path forward. I felt that Ray McMillan, who's Black, would be wise to take my counsel. Impatiently, I felt we should focus far less on the pain and impact the interactions had on Ray and instead look at ways to bring strategic change. In retrospect, I wanted to move on too quickly and not allow time for healing. When Ray insisted that we slow down and address the pain, wounds, and broken relationships first, I stepped away for a season. My stubborn inability to follow Black leadership and lack of compassion and empathy for how all this was affecting Ray personally only added to the pain.

A few years later, a major Christian conference was coming to Cincinnati, and they had asked Pastor Ray to be the local chairperson. Ray had never stopped pushing pastors and leaders to address racism, and this led to some unresolved tension among pastors and church leaders in Cincinnati. I was concerned these conflicts would get in the way of Ray's leadership at this national conference.

Instead of bringing my concerns directly to Ray, I shared them with a friend, who then shared them with the organization, which then rescinded its invitation to Ray to be the local chair. I had played a major role in this decision by failing to be honest about my concerns with Ray and instead attempting to orchestrate outcomes in the shadows.

When Ray found out, he confronted me. While I went through a period of self-justification, I eventually recognized the damage I had done and worked to make amends. Thankfully, Ray didn't give up on me. Instead, he agreed to keep walking with me, holding me accountable, and pushing me to be more like Jesus. Through Ray, I learned that my instinct to center my White perspective is always dormant in my mind and heart, threatening to keep me stagnant. Without diligence and a reliance on God to guide me, it can come back in an instant.

Over the past fifteen years, as I've grown in my awareness and relationship with not only Ray but also other incredible Black friends and leaders, I've stumbled over this impulse to control more often than I'd like to admit. And to me, the ugly presence of racism is most real in my heart and life because of my implicit and subconscious feelings of superiority.

Thankfully, there's a path toward redemption—but not through cheap grace. No, this comes only through the amazing grace that expects and demands confession, repentance, and deep, invasive open-heart surgery. Over time, I began to see that Ray was tired of soft selling the brutal realities of racism to ease the consciences of White leaders at the expense of truth and justice.

Learning to Follow Black Leadership

In the late 1990s, I returned to school to pursue a PhD in US history with a focus on civil rights at the University of Kentucky. My advisor, Dr. Gerald Smith, had just been invited by Dr. Clayborne Carson, director of the Martin Luther King, Jr. Papers Project, to be an editor for a volume of King's early religious writings and sermons. Dr. Smith asked me to be his graduate assistant on the project, and eventually I was invited to also be an editor.

My time with the King papers led me to a deep appreciation of the sacrifice and struggle necessary, by both Dr. King and countless others whose names we may not know, to bring racial justice. But my studies and my role as an editor with the King papers also meant I felt like I had less time for local engagement, particularly in the days, weeks, and months following major unrest in Cincinnati in 2001, which had a deep impact on both Chuck and me.

Over the course of five years, Cincinnati police killed fifteen Black men and women, culminating in the death of unarmed teenager Timothy Thomas in April 2001. One of the deaths that set the stage, however, was the suffocation of Roger Owensby Jr. in November 2000. An officer had accused Owensby of theft a few days earlier, and police detained him outside a convenience store questioning him for around fifteen minutes, at which point he apparently got scared and tried to flee. Police quickly took him to the ground, choked him, and piled on him. After several minutes, they put him in the back seat of a police cruiser facedown with the heat on full blast and the motor running as the officers tried to get their story straight on what had transpired. Owensby died of suffocation.

There were other questionable deaths as well, including the shooting of mental health patient Lorenzo Collins in 1997. Collins, who many believed should have been in a mental health facility instead of on the streets, threatened surrounding officers with a brick. He was otherwise unarmed. One of the officers shot and killed Collins.

Given the frustration and anger at the police force from many in the Black community, the Thomas killing became a spark for unrest. A few neighborhoods in the city experienced violence over several days. Finally, our mayor imposed a curfew on the city, but it was selectively enforced in Black neighborhoods.

Soon our phone started ringing off the hook, as friends and family called to check in. A few friends from the suburbs offered to let us stay with them for a few days until things settled down. We politely declined all these offers. During the curfew, we sat on our porch, as did many of our neighbors, checking in on each other. At the time, I couldn't imagine feeling any safer than my family and I felt as White people in the middle of a Black neighborhood.

Before the unrest, the Cincinnati Black United Front (a coalition of activists and clergy) and the ACLU had filed a lawsuit against the Cincinnati Police Department for racial profiling. When an officer killed Timothy Thomas, the Black United Front, led by Reverend Damon Lynch III of New Prospect Baptist Church, played a pivotal role in the response. They called for an economic boycott of the city. They continued to pursue their lawsuit. They engaged in regular public meetings and actions. They took the heat of those in power who viewed the Black United Front as too radical. But leaders like Reverend Lynch and Iris Roley offered courageous and determined leadership during a critical moment for our city.

Eventually, their work resulted in a model collaborative agreement between the US Justice Department, the local Fraternal Order of Police, the city of Cincinnati, and the Black United Front that reshaped policing in our city. Problem-solving together—between community members, public officials, and the police—became the standard.

In the days, weeks, and months following the unrest, I continued to have comfortable meetings with my evangelical clergy friends, Black and White, who weren't aligned with Reverend Lynch and the Black United Front. During the week of the unrest, I finally attended a meeting where Reverend Lynch was speaking, and I felt like I was hearing a clear call for justice that resonated deeply in my spirit. But when a few of my fellow clergy decided to leave the meeting because they felt Reverend Lynch's approach was too confrontational, I left too. My heart still sinks today when I think about that choice I made more than two decades ago.

Years later, when I became the executive director of a local faith-based organization called the AMOS Project, I saw Reverend Lynch at a local rally for racial justice. I went up to him and, in an act of repentance, confessed my regret for not following his leadership thirteen years earlier. I then committed to support him in any way I could in the months and years ahead. Reverend Lynch ended up joining the board of the AMOS Project, and in our final year in Cincinnati before my family and I moved to Columbus in late 2017, we were members of his church, New Prospect Baptist.

Despite my commitment to always show up for racial justice, I missed a chance in 2001 to be a part of an amazing move of God. I could come up with all sorts of reasons why—I was busy with my studies and pastoring and family. But ultimately, I lacked the courage to follow my convictions. I was not yet willing to follow Black leadership. I lost an opportunity to learn from and work alongside amazing Black leaders. Thankfully, years later, I had a chance to act differently, to heal and grow, and to be part of the movement for Black lives, where I got to be part of struggles for justice with Reverend Lynch, Iris Roley, Ray McMillan, and Chuck.

Owning up to misses in the past opened new opportunities for me. Over the years, I realized that being a good friend across race was not about me being perfect, but rather about me being engaged and humble and staying in the struggle. I also learned that I can easily become stagnant and distant and, in my complacency, sometimes miss God's call. The consistent invitation from the Holy Spirit and my friends of Color is to reengage despite my failures, misses, and mistakes.

You've probably heard the phrase "I just need to get back to my roots." This rootedness in our stories, including events and relationships that shaped us, and those times when we have made mistakes give us grounding to confidently join the movement for racial healing, solidarity, and justice.

We all have the opportunity to get back to our roots. Our deepest, truest roots. We share a common identity as children of God. This shared humanity, filled with unique and common experiences, prepares us to love courageously together.

One of the greatest blessings of my life over the past few decades has been learning from and partnering with BIPOC friends and colleagues. I recall those who have helped me grow along the journey, like Wilmot Allen, Ray McMillan, Reverend Damon Lynch III, and many others. I appreciate their patience and love, and how they challenged me to reflect on how hard it was to be openhearted and see my own arrogance along the way. They and many others have helped me grow in love and action.

None of these relationships, and the blessings they are in my life, would be possible without continuing to remember and reflect on my story, including my fumbling but learning along the way, so God can bring healing and restoration.

EXAMINE YOUR STORY

1. How does your Jesus story inform your race story?

2. Reflect on the first time you were aware of race. How old were you? What feeling do you associate with that first experience and why?

3. What are three to five significant events from your life that have shaped you and your perspectives on race? Were these events seasons of stagnancy or flow? We invite you to spend some time journaling and praying about these memories. What might God be saying to you about your past, present, and future?

PART 2

REALIZE

WALK HUMBLY

1. ROOT

2. REALIZE—Confronting the broader story of race in the United States.

When Nehemiah's brother brought news that Jerusalem's city walls and gates had been destroyed by fire, this was Nehemiah's reaction:

When I heard these words, I sat down and wept and mourned for days, fasting and praying before the God of heaven. (Neh. 1:4)

When we face tragedy, our emotions vary. Some people may get angry. Some may turn introspective. Nehemiah wept, and lament is an important way we can respond to a broken world.

Nehemiah entered the UNDIVIDED Circle. He had started his journey of walking humbly through rooting his identity in being a child of God. Nehemiah was concerned for the Jews because he understood that when any of God's people were in trouble, he was in trouble too. Because we're connected. Because we're part of a holy family.

So Nehemiah sat. He did not act. He sat. He paused. He took a beat to reflect—to wrap his mind around the horrendous state his brothers and sisters were in. He'd asked the right question, and now he needed to process the answer.

One of the distinctives in our seven-session experience, and in all the group experiences we lead, is making time for pausing and reflecting. We see that Nehemiah didn't spring to action out of his emotions but first took time to make room for the range of emotions he was feeling. This often-neglected personal step—pausing, reflecting, and feeling—is essential to the long-term work of racial healing and justice.

Instead of shaking his finger and assigning blame, Nehemiah wept. He mourned for days, fasting and praying before the God of heaven.

Examine the words of Nehemiah's prayer:

I now pray before you day and night for your servants, the Israelites, confessing the sins of the Israelites, which we have sinned against you. Both I and my family have sinned. We have offended you deeply, failing to keep the commandments, the statutes, and the ordinances that you commanded Moses your servant. (1:6–7)

After pausing to consider the news his brother had given him, Nehemiah prayed a prayer of repentance—not just for the forgiveness of others, but for his own sinfulness. "Both I and my family have sinned." Nehemiah had a moment of realization: *I'm part of the problem.* He took ownership for any part he'd had in the suffering of the survivors. Wow.

Nehemiah believed another path was possible because it had happened before. Nehemiah knew the God of Abraham, Sarah, and Hagar, the God of Joseph, and the God of the exodus was more than able to bring restoration. Looking backward, Nehemiah recognized two things. He knew the pain of that present moment was due to rebellion against God and a disregard for God's people created in God's image. He also realized that, as we're tethered to God's love and power, we're invited to be part of God's redemption and restoration in the most desperate circumstances.

Nehemiah's reaction to his brother's report of the trouble they were in came from asking two simple questions:

1. What's my role in the trouble we're in?
2. How can I be an active part of the solution?

Nehemiah entered the second step in the UNDIVIDED Circle.

Step Two: Realize

Being rooted is critical to taking the next step: realize.

When we're clear on who we are, our identity in Christ, we can then effectively and fully realize our current circumstances and the role we're being called to play in changing them.

Realization demands examination. It's a habit that's developed over time. It may not come naturally to you, and it may be uncomfortable at first. But the ability to honestly examine your reaction and introspectively consider what role you can play in the problem's resolution will be the measure of your ability to walk in humility to accomplish what is good.

There are also moments of inspiration in the story of race and faith in America. This mixed and complex story is where we will turn next.

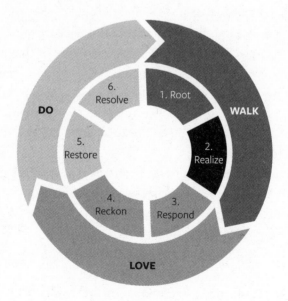

3   Hope in History

One of our (Chuck and Troy's) favorite movies is *Remember the Titans*. Sure, it's pure Hollywood, with all the expected melodramatic scenes, and right on cue we have shed our fair share of tears while watching this film. Why do we love it? Based on a true story, the movie follows a football team dealing with intense racial strife in the early 1970s. Over the course of the film, the coach convinces the team to embrace solidarity across races, and the team goes on to win the championship.

We also love the title: *Remember the Titans*.

What we remember matters, and what we forget matters.

To live undivided, remembering our past (including the messy parts) can get us moving in the right direction. The Old Testament includes many titan moments, like the exodus and parting of the Red Sea, the walls tumbling down in Jericho, and David slaying Goliath, while also not pulling any punches on the less savory parts of the story that ultimately led to the downfall of Jerusalem and decades in exile.

We also know we can find hope in history as we pay attention to some of the followers of Jesus who demonstrated what's possible when we embody courageous love.

We remember the Titans because they were the exception— a team coming together across racial differences in the early 1970s was far from the norm. At the time (and even today), far too many teams, schools, and cities were divided by race and ethnicity.

Amid the unsavory aspects of the American story, there have always been titans—those who help us find hope in history. Let's turn our gaze to some of these stories that bring us hope.

New Richmond

At our UNDIVIDED team retreat in September 2022, we did a walking tour of an unassuming river town about twenty miles east of Cincinnati called New Richmond, just a few miles from Troy's home. New Richmond sits in Clermont County, which was 95 percent White in the 2020 US Census.

In the middle of the nineteenth century, New Richmond, and particularly the congregations of the town, stood tall supporting the Underground Railroad and advancing abolitionism. Given the city's proximity to the slave state of Kentucky across the Ohio River, several New Richmond homes were vital parts of the Underground Railroad. The city also became a bastion for anti-slavery zeal.

One New Richmond titan worth remembering is Amos Dresser. When he was in his late twenties, Dresser attended Lane Seminary in Cincinnati. He was there in early 1834 for the Lane Seminary debates, critical conversations on the biblical and theological grounding for and against American slavery. These controversial conversations, which were the first public debates on the abolition of slavery, added momentum to the abolition movement. They were attended by famous abolitionists like John Rankin and influenced *Uncle Tom's Cabin* author Harriet Beecher Stowe. Months later, when Lane Seminary trustees passed a resolution banning abolitionist groups from campus, Dresser was part of the Lane Rebels, who left the school in protest. Many went on to a new school in northern Ohio called Oberlin College, which embraced abolitionism and was led for a period by evangelist Charles Grandison Finney.

But Dresser went south, heading to Mississippi and then Tennessee to sell Bibles and promote abolitionism, for which he was arrested in Memphis during the summer of 1835. Local officials sentenced Dresser to a public lashing, which they carried out by striking him at least twenty times in the town square. Those who sentenced Dresser suggested their harsh punishment was intended to save him, a White man, from being lynched. Following this beating, with his life in jeopardy, Dresser headed north, and a few years later became pastor of First Presbyterian Church in New Richmond.

In 1836, First Presbyterian began holding meetings of the New Richmond Anti-Slavery Society and made a declaration to sever relationships with any congregation that supported slavery. During this period, the church hosted leading voices of the anti-slavery movement, including James G. Birney, John Rankin, Calvin Stowe and George Beecher (the husband and brother of Harriet Beecher Stowe, respectively).

Dresser and First Presbyterian were part of a larger mosaic of Jesus followers fighting against slavery and working for justice in New Richmond. In early 1836, James Birney launched an important anti-slavery newspaper, *The Philanthropist*, in the town. Under constant threat from pro-slavery forces, a few citizens of the city formed the Chieftains of Liberty, which organized nightly armed vigils to protect the paper's printing press.

Before the Civil War, New Richmond also had a robust Free Black community, which established Second Baptist Church, and in 1857 launched the Union for the Advancement of Colored Men of New Richmond, an organization "desirous of employing all means in our power for the elevation of ourselves and community and race."[1] The National Association for the Advancement of Colored People, or NAACP, with similar aims at a national level, didn't launch until fifty-two years later, in 1909. The Black community made up roughly 20 percent of New Richmond's population into the early twentieth century, when manufacturing jobs in larger cities led many to leave. Still, remnants of this vibrant Black community, animated by faith and a passion for equity and justice, continue to this day.[2]

Berea College

Another story of bold Christian leadership took place just south of Lexington, Kentucky, with the founding of Berea College. Just a few years before the start of the Civil War, abolitionist John G. Fee founded the school as the first fully integrated and one of the first coeducational colleges in the South. He hoped for a school that would be "antislavery, anti-caste, anti-rum, anti-sin."[3] The school's commitment to racial justice showed up in bold countercultural leadership like its 1872 decision to allow interracial dating. In the latter years of the nineteenth century, against the backdrop of increased segregation, growing violence targeting Black people, and the rise of lynching, Berea College stood firm in its commitment to its original school slogan taken from the King James Version of Acts 17:26: "And hath made of one blood all nations of men."

For the school's first several decades, it had a fairly equal mix of Black and White students. This changed in 1904, when Carl Day of the Kentucky House of Representatives trumpeted the passage of a bill originally called "An Act to Prohibit White and Colored Persons from Attending the Same School." The bill became law in the state, but Berea College didn't back away from its Christian commitment to integration and appealed the law all the way to the US Supreme Court in a case known as *Berea College v. Kentucky* (1908). The court sided with the state of Kentucky, so for the next four decades, Berea continued as an all-White college but also started a new all-Black school near Louisville called the Lincoln Institute. In 1950, as soon as the law changed in Kentucky, Berea College returned to its roots as an integrated college.

Part of titan John G. Fee's legacy through Berea College is the story of one of its most celebrated alums who's a titan in his own right. In 1903, just a year before Kentucky lawmakers mandated that Berea College become segregated, Carter G. Woodson earned his bachelor's degree from the school. Woodson is considered by many to be the "father of Black history." In 1916, he started the *Journal of Negro History* and a decade later initiated the observance of the first Black History Week. In 1970, Black History Week became Black History Month, which we continue to celebrate every February in the United States.

Montgomery, Alabama

Perhaps a more familiar story of true titans in the struggle for racial justice is Montgomery, Alabama, from 1955 to 1956. Here a group of Christian women, known as the Women's Political Council, launched a bus boycott that would reshape the city and a nation. Mary Fair Burks, a member of Dexter Avenue Baptist Church, got the idea to found a women's organization during a sermon by Reverend Vernon Johns, who often challenged his congregation to do more in the struggle for justice and equity. Burks recruited Jo Ann Robinson, an English professor at Alabama State College, an HBCU (Historically Black College or University) in the heart of Montgomery.

Robinson became president of the Women's Political Council, and when she heard of Rosa Parks's arrest on December 1, 1955, she sprang into action. Robinson quickly typed out a call for a one-day bus boycott for the following Monday, December 5, on mimeograph paper, and then proceeded to crank out hundreds of flyers. She also put her network into action, getting dozens of Black women to flood the Black community with the notices. The following day, a reluctant Dr. Martin Luther King Jr. decided to support the boycott, and the community elected him president of the Montgomery Improvement Association. Over the following year, Black Jesus followers in Montgomery demonstrated resilience and courage and put faith into action daily to love one another and advance the cause of racial justice.

In a prescient close to his speech on the first night of the boycott, King shared these words to a standing-room-only crowd at Holt Street Baptist Church:

> As we stand and sit here this evening and as we prepare ourselves for what lies ahead, let us go out with a grim and bold determination that we are going to stick together. We are going to work together. Right here in Montgomery, when the history books are written in the future, somebody will have to say, "There lived a race of people, a black people, 'fleecy locks and black complexion,' a people who had the moral courage to stand up for their rights. And thereby they injected a new meaning into the veins of history and of civilization." And we're gonna do that. God grant that we will do it before it is too late.[4]

Today the history books do indeed remember these titans, but not just Martin Luther King Jr. and Rosa Parks, and not just Ralph David Abernathy and Jo Ann Robinson. We also recall the White people of Montgomery who stood in solidarity throughout the boycott: Pastor Robert Graetz and his wife,

Jean; Clifford and Virginia Durr; and others. Most significantly, we remember the fifty thousand Black titans who boycotted buses for over 380 days so God's kingdom would be more fully realized on this earth.[5]

Cesar Chavez

During the Lenten season of 1966, another group led by Jesus followers called the nation to justice. Several months earlier, farmworkers in Delano, California, decided to go on strike against local grape vineyard owners, seeking better pay and working conditions. The protest brought together Filipino Americans and Mexican Americans, who stood in solidarity. Cesar Chavez, a committed Catholic and seasoned community organizer, led the effort. As the strike and accompanying nascent boycott of table grapes were losing steam, Chavez and his leaders from the National Farm Workers Association and the Agricultural Workers Organizing Committee called for a three hundred–mile pilgrimage from Delano to the state capital in Sacramento to correspond with the Lenten season.

In announcing the pilgrimage of "Peregrinacion, Penitencia, Revolucion" or "Pilgrimage, Penance, and Revolution," Chavez appealed to the long history of pilgrimage and public penance, wherein people

> would march through the streets, often in sack cloth and ashes, some even carrying crosses, as a sign of penance for their sins, and as a plan for the mercy of God. The penitential procession is also in the blood of the Mexican-American, and the Delano march will therefore be one of penance—public penance for the sins of the strikers, their own personal sins as well as their yielding perhaps to feelings of hatred and revenge in the strike

97

itself. They hope by the march to set themselves at peace with the Lord, so that the justice of their cause will be purified of all lesser motivation.[6]

This Jesus-centered approach made their calls for justice even more poignant, as Chavez noted that for the Mexican American, "Delano is his 'cause,' his great demand for justice, freedom, and respect from a predominantly foreign cultural community in a land where he was first. The revolutions of Mexico were primarily uprisings of the poor, fighting for bread and for dignity. The Mexican-American is also a child of the revolution."[7] In calling out "a land where he was first," Chavez recognized the levels of injustice of many of the farmworkers, whose ancestors included Native Americans who lived on and farmed these lands long before White settlers came to present-day California. Also, while leaning into penance, Chavez did not shy away from the rich legacy of fighting for justice that his people embodied.

On March 17, more than fifty farmworkers began the three hundred–mile journey to Sacramento, with supporters joining the pilgrimage along the way. Many farmers joined for a few minutes, a few miles, or a few hours. By the time they reached the state capital, during Holy Week, the growing power of the pilgrimage helped the workers secure their first union contract with an owner of one of the local vineyards. On April 10, 1966, Easter Sunday, over eight thousand people marched in Sacramento, led by farmworkers. Dolores Huerta, one of the emerging leaders of the farmworkers, gave a rousing speech at the capital:

We are not alone. We are accompanied by many friends. The religious leaders of the state, spear-headed by the migrant ministry, the student groups, the civil rights groups that make up the movement that has been successful in securing civil rights for Negroes in this country, right-thinking citizens and our staunchest ally, organized labor, are all in the revolution of the farm worker.[8]

The migrant ministry, which continues today as the National Farm Worker Ministry, began as a Christian organization in the 1920s, offering direct aid and support to poor and struggling migrant workers in the United States. Around the time of the pilgrimage, the migrant ministry added a commitment to justice for the farmworker as an essential part of its mission. On Easter Sunday 1966, the migrant ministry committed to the revolution of the farmworker, which meant being treated with dignity and not being consigned to poverty level wages.

The strike and accompanying boycott of table grapes lasted several more years. Finally, in 1970, the union signed a contract with the growers of Delano, California, that meant better wages and working conditions for the farmers. Cesar Chavez, the migrant ministry, and most significantly the farmworkers themselves were true titans in this struggle for justice.

Chinatown Rising

In the fall of 2022, the two of us joined a weeklong Asian American Civil Rights pilgrimage through California led by Andrew Kim of Kensington Church in Michigan. We confronted our nation's troubling anti-Asian story along the way, including the Chinese Exclusion Act of 1882; the immigration law of 1924, which made it almost impossible for Asians to immigrate to the United States; and the decision to incarcerate 110,000 Japanese, many of whom were US citizens, during World War II.

Often Asian American communities are tagged as the "model minority" by our society. The connotation of this term implies that unlike other Black, Indigenous, and People of Color, those of Asian descent have seemingly been able to assimilate. It also suggests that if one simply applies oneself, through grit and personal responsibility, the American Dream is achievable. But this moniker hides more difficult truths. One is that the Asian American and Pacific Islander community is not a monolith.

Portland, Oregon, for example, contains two large Asian American enclaves. One in the Beaverton area largely consists of wealthier people who are connected with Nike and the tech industry, and the other is in the city of Portland and is made up of more recent immigrants and refugees who tend to be working class, struggling to get by day to day. There are also vast differences based on country of origin, as the experiences of Chinese or Japanese communities may differ vastly from those from Laos or Cambodia.

On the last day of the learning experience, we saw *Chinatown Rising*, a documentary by Josh Chuck chronicling a twenty-five-year struggle for justice and opportunity for the largely Chinese American residents of Chinatown in the heart of San Francisco. Chinese immigration to the West Coast accelerated as labor needs grew with the expansion of railways in the mid-1800s. Once the transcontinental railroad was complete, and the perceived need for cheap Chinese labor decreased, anti-Asian rhetoric and laws sprung up, culminating in the Chinese Exclusion Act of 1882. In response, Asian ethnicities sought protection and identity in urban enclaves like Little Tokyo in Los Angeles and Chinatowns in Los Angeles and San Francisco. When a major earthquake and fires devastated San Francisco in 1906, developers saw an opportunity to displace Chinatown, moving the Chinese community several miles south of the heart of the city. Before these plans took root, Chinese immigrants immediately started rebuilding on some of the highest-valued land in not only San Francisco but the entire world, preventing developers from seizing their land.

Long before an earthquake reshaped San Francisco, the Presbyterian Church established Cameron House in the heart of Chinatown to provide a safe haven for Chinese women, who were often trafficked and sexually exploited. Over the years, the ministry embodied Jesus's love and concern for new immigrants to the United States. Increasingly, in the 1970s and 80s, under the leadership of Chinese American pastor Harry Chuck, the organization got more and more involved in fighting for justice for their community, securing over four thousand neighborhood signatures to prevent a developer from turning an important playground into a parking garage. Later, Pastor Chuck led a movement that lasted several years to get resources from the US Department of Housing and Urban Development (HUD) to a new apartment building in the community, which includes over 150 units of affordable senior housing. The 2019 documentary *Chinatown Rising* demonstrates the vital role that Christian leadership played in protecting Chinatown and its residents and in advancing racial justice.

As we remember these titans, we must not gloss over some of the uglier parts of our nation's story, from the genocide and forced relocation of Native Americans to the trafficking, enslavement, and lynching of Black Americans. Over the centuries, this dehumanization has extended to immigrants from Ireland and Eastern Europe, and with increasing vitriol and impact toward Asian and Latin American immigrants.

Like the prayer of Nehemiah, which opened this chapter, parts of our shared story demand our acknowledgment, reckoning, lament, and repentance.

As 2019 approached, marking the four-hundredth anniversary of the first enslaved Africans arriving in what would become the United States of America, Nikole Hannah-Jones of the *New York Times* launched the 1619 Project to remember and tell stories that are often forgotten or hidden in history books. In response to this series, a debate emerged about whether to center 1619 or 1776 when telling this nation's story.

We both grew up in schools where 1776 was a primary focus, and you probably did too. We didn't hear anything about 1619 and why it mattered. We celebrate July 4, 1776, as a major holiday, with fireworks, American flags, and barbecues full of patriotic-themed desserts featuring strawberries, blueberries, and whipped topping. July 4 is not going away. There's no danger of 1776 being erased from our collective memory. This is for good reason—the Declaration of Independence and the revolutionary era produced a form of government, the Bill of Rights, and a nation with laudable principles that Martin Luther King Jr. cited during his famous "I Have a Dream" speech nearly two centuries later.

At the same time, whether the year is 1619 or 1776 or any year in our shared history, the full truth still comes through. Pick any year, and the story will include titans and racism. This nation declared independence from Britain while denying independence to enslaved Black people. That's part of the legacy of 1776 and our nation.

Remember, there's always a remnant. Just as God, in the days of Elijah, reserved seven thousand who had not bowed to false gods, so there are always faithful people, including those who joined the struggle for racial justice during times of horrific racial injustice.

These simple stories—of Amos Dresser and the titans of New Richmond, Ohio; John G. Fee and Carter Woodson of

Berea College; Jo Ann Robinson and the heroes of Montgomery, Alabama; Cesar Chavez, the migrant ministry, and the farmworkers of California; and Pastor Harry Chuck and the courageous people of Chinatown in San Francisco—show us over and over again that another path is possible. When we live undivided, we follow a great cloud of witnesses who have gone before us.

4 Stagnant Roots

The people of Jerusalem were in trouble because of centuries of sin, injustice, and devastation. Walls don't just fall down. Things are broken for a reason. This is true for us as well.

Okay, be honest—what cities come to mind when you think of communities in trouble? Maybe you think of cities you associate with crime and poverty. Chances are, the cities that come to mind first have a substantial BIPOC population.

That is true in the Midwest, where cities like Flint (Michigan), Gary (Indiana), and Youngstown in our home state of Ohio have come to symbolize despair. If you know Ohio, you may also think of East Liverpool, a largely White Appalachian town on the Ohio River in the shadows of one of the world's largest toxic waste incinerators. The toxic train derailment that made national news in early 2023 was just up the river from East Liverpool. The town has some of the highest cancer rates in the nation. These former industrial powerhouse cities and river towns are now shells of their former selves. We all see the trouble they are in.

Depending on the part of the country you live in, the composition of poorer and largely neglected neighborhoods and cities may change, with some having more people of Latin American, Indigenous, Asian, or Appalachian descent. No matter where you live, however, massive disparities across race and class mark every region and every state in these United States, and cities are often left in the wake.

How did we get here? How did the walls fall?

One aspect of the UNDIVIDED experience is the opportunity to dig deeper and explore further through what we call "activation assignments." These opportunities allow you to customize your learning journey, letting your curiosity guide new insights. With that in mind, we've built a few activation assignments into this chapter. Take the time to complete one or more of these. They will help the information you read resonate more with your local context.

A Shaky Foundation

For at least four hundred years, people on this land have struggled with the impact and legacy of racism. The majority of us lament the eras of slavery, segregation, and lynching that mark our shared story. But haven't we made a lot of progress over the past few hundred years, and especially over the past few decades? Fundamental to the American ideal is the notion that with hard work, any person can make it. This is often called the American Dream. Everyone has a shot. In the nineteenth century, Horatio Alger popularized stories of young men who, despite humble beginnings and through tenacity and good works, achieved success in the US. These "rags to riches" and "pull yourselves up by your bootstraps" stories continue to undergird many of the personal responsibility narratives that are pervasive in our society and in the church. Is it not true that all of us have an equal opportunity to succeed and thrive in this nation?

We are all called to be good stewards of our lives, our talents, and our gifts. To suggest we have no agency or no personal responsibility is destructive and denies the God-given dignity and potential that are ours as image bearers.

Upon closer evaluation, however, these "rags to riches" stories erase very real and historically rooted barriers that mark our society and conspire together either for one's success or for one's failure. Interlocking systems of education, housing, transportation, health care, wealth, and employment have largely favored White males in the United States and continue to do so today. This isn't to say there aren't very real socioeconomic distinctions within the White population as well, and across gender, but to be Black, Brown, or Person of Color has carried with it a stigma and fewer opportunities—which have contributed to divergent outcomes.

If systemic racism doesn't exist, how do we explain the disparate inequities in the data between races that both historically and perpetually mark the American experience? If systemic injustice isn't real, the only other viable option is to make the case that Black, Indigenous, and other People of Color are inferior to the dominant White culture. Or we can just say it plainly: White people and/or White culture is superior.

In the twenty-first century, most wouldn't be so blatant as to claim White people are simply better than Black, Indigenous, and other People of Color. But code words or talking around the statistics don't make the import any different. The implied superiority of Western thought—the call to "civilize" people who are not of European descent, the idea that the United States is superior and ordained by God—makes subtle appeals to the inherent supremacy of White Western and European culture.

Based on the facts, either systemic racism exists or White is the superior race. So, which is it?

Does systemic racism exist? If it does, how does it show up? Let's look at how it manifests itself in three ways: restricting movement, narrowing opportunity, and minimizing voice.

Systemic Racism Restricts Movement

Restricting movement isolates and denies us from hearing each other's stories and recognizing the common humanity in one another. Restricting movement gives way to control at all costs, which limits listening, understanding, and change. Restricting movement is stagnancy.

It's also at the core of slavery wherever it takes place—claiming to own another human being gives one a distorted authority to set limits on where that other person can and cannot go. In the US, slave patrols emerged to enforce this restriction, and courageous individuals like Harriet Tubman built the Underground Railroad to resist this restriction.

Once slavery ended, freedom of movement for formerly enslaved people led to the Great Migration, a several-decades-long flow of millions of Black people from the South to the Northeast, Midwest, and West during the twentieth century. But the end of slavery did not end attempts to restrict the movement of Black and Brown people in this country. Segregation laws limited where Black people could sit, stand, eat, sleep, drink, swim, and use the restroom. Theaters and churches prevented Black people from the best seats, or even entrance into the building.

The most insidious restrictions of movement limited where people could live because of their race, ethnicity, or heritage. The US government forcibly removed Indigenous tribes, restricting them to smaller and smaller parcels of undesirable land, largely in the plains and deserts of the Western United

States. Reservations are a manifestation of systemic racism that restrict movement. During World War II, the US government also set up internment camps and imprisoned over one hundred thousand Japanese Americans because of their racial and ethnic identity.

We recently visited one of these camps in Manzanar, California, where the US government incarcerated over a thousand American citizens of Japanese descent and Japanese immigrants for over three years during World War II. On the day we visited the poorly constructed barracks, the wind and cold were so uncomfortable that our group of ten sprinted from one structure to another during the tour. As we read about the conditions of the barracks and how untreated wood was used to build them, causing the gaping holes between the slats, it was sobering to imagine how men, women, and children carried on. These families, who through the period of incarceration often lost all their worldly goods, were also stripped of their dignity and their rights as law-abiding Americans.

During the Great Migration, housing restrictions became a matter of course in cities throughout the nation. A majority of new homes and neighborhoods constructed to meet the demands in growing cities stipulated that only White people could live in them. Racial covenants, or restrictions due to race on home deeds in certain neighborhoods, were common throughout the first half of the twentieth century. Though deemed unconstitutional in 1948, the practice did not end.[1] In our hometown of Cincinnati, one of our Black friends and a cofounder of UNDIVIDED, Charla Weiss, found remnants of this language when she and her White husband bought a home in the city in the 1980s, and the contract stated that the property could not be sold, leased, rented to, or occupied by non-Whites.

Despite the legal ruling to end the practice, White-only neighborhoods remained a matter of course for most of the latter half of the twentieth century, largely through neighborhood associations, intimidation, and even violence. This was true in the Cincinnati area, where the neighborhood of Clifton remained a predominantly White community because of the power of the Clifton Town Meeting, which was established in 1961 to keep Clifton a "desirable neighborhood," a subtle phrase that implied "White only."[2]

As early as the 1930s, banks began to offer home loans with 20 percent down and a thirty-year term, but only to those living in neighborhoods that were deemed lower risk to the lending institution. Having Black and Brown people in the community was a quick way for it to get "redlined" and thus determined as too high-risk to get a home loan, lowering home ownership rates, property values, and wealth accumulation in neighborhoods of Color around the nation.

The GI Bill, offered to veterans of World War II, offered low-interest mortgages and school tuition. These benefits proved elusive for many Black veterans, however, who had difficulty securing these loans and getting access to tuition assistance. The benefits disproportionately benefited White veterans and their families. In the US, where generational wealth and access to capital is often tied up in home ownership, the ripples of disparities in the implementation of the GI bill continue through today.

As new interstate highways began carving up traditional Black and Brown neighborhoods in cities around the US, Black residents needed restrictions lifted so they could find adequate housing. Early efforts by Black families to move into new neighborhoods often depended on blockbusting. Under this scheme, real estate agents bought a home in an all-White neighborhood at an above-market rate and then surreptitiously sold it to a Black family. Once the sale was complete, the agents would make phone calls and go door-to-door in the neighborhood, announcing that the community was integrating and their property values were about to plummet. Panic selling ensued, with White families selling homes below market value to real estate brokers who then flipped these same houses to Black families for a nice profit. In the case of blockbusting, movement may have been possible, but only by price gouging Black and Brown people for profit and capitalizing on the fear of White households.

Over the past several decades, the number of people incarcerated in this country has grown exponentially. A large driver has been the War on Drugs, an approach that was touted to make neighborhoods safer but ended up being used to disproportionately imprison Black and Brown people. Meanwhile, the cash bail system means those with limited economic resources awaiting trial remain in jail regardless of flight risk or public safety. As a result, the United States has become the most incarcerated nation in the world and US jails and prisons disproportionately restrict the movement of Black and Brown people.

In all its forms, restricting movement creates stagnancy, a pattern that continues to shape our American experience.

Activation Assignment

Look around at your city, state, or region. Where do you see the signs of restricted movement shaping your environment? Research the Indigenous tribes that once occupied the city or state where you currently live. How did the restriction of movement affect Indigenous tribes that once lived in your area? Are there any public acknowledgements or recognition of their history and contributions?

Systemic Racism Narrows Opportunity

Another insidious way race plays out in our society is by narrowing opportunities for Black, Brown, Indigenous, and immigrant communities. Far too often and for far too long, one's race or ethnicity has restricted opportunity. As a society, we routinely recognize this by highlighting "firsts"—the first Black man to play Major League Baseball (Jackie Robinson), the first Black man to serve on the Supreme Court (Thurgood Marshall), the first Black woman in space (Mae Jemison), the first Asian American woman elected to the US Congress (Patsy Mink), the first Latin American senator (Octaviano Ambrosio Larrazolo), or the first Native American in space (John Herrington). These firsts matter because they break a pattern of leadership and opportunity that has been marked by Whiteness. The reason we mark firsts is that limited opportunity functions throughout society, beginning with education.

Limiting education started during slavery. By the 1830s, most slave states had passed laws making it illegal for enslaved individuals to read and write. Following emancipation, the Freedmen's Bureau, a US government program, marshaled resources to fund education for those formerly enslaved, though more schools were founded and led by Black people themselves. But the Southern states did not demonstrate a strong commitment to educating Black citizens, and segregated, separate, underfunded, and unequal schools marked not only the South but also much of the nation until the landmark *Brown v. Board of Education* decision in 1954, which deemed separate but equal unconstitutional.

But the Supreme Court's decision has not resulted in educational equity. In the immediate aftermath, many White Southerners vacated the public schools. Some established private

Christian schools, not primarily because they wanted prayer in school or to make sure their children were shaped by Christian values, but because they did not want their children attending school with Black students.

In the twenty-first century, the disparities in education remain. Property values reflect it. Parents make decisions about where to live based on the quality of schools. While the reasons are complex, as recently as 2016, students in wealthier and Whiter school districts can be as many as four grade levels ahead of poorer districts with higher numbers of Black and Brown children.[3] In fact, in a landmark 2002 ruling, the Ohio Supreme Court ruled that the state's method for funding public school education (mainly through property taxes that favor wealthy neighborhoods) was unconstitutional on four separate occasions, but a remedy remains elusive decades later.[4]

It's a good thing parents want to give their kids the best education possible. We all do. It's even better when a parent can actually give their child the best education possible. The right response is not to feel guilty if your kids have opportunities. Rather, it is to feel driven to help others of different races or ethnicities have these opportunities as well.

Both of us had our opportunities expanded through education. I (Troy) attended school in a district filled with engineers and mathematicians connected to General Motors plants in town. When I was a senior, I entered a math contest at Franklin College in Indiana and took home first place, which included a full-tuition, four-year scholarship. While this was in part due to my math ability, it cannot be separated from my context: I attended the best high school in a good school district, with math teachers who also taught regularly at the college level. Side note: don't ask me for help with math today—all my skill is gone!

113

Meanwhile, my (Chuck's) private school elementary education expanded my opportunities to attend a fantastic college preparatory magnet school in Philadelphia. In turn, *that* opened college possibilities and propelled me down a path that led to a great job at Procter & Gamble, a *Fortune* 100 company, straight out of college.

Expanded opportunities create flow, while narrowed opportunities reinforce stagnancy.

Activation Assignment

Here's a challenge. Go to this link from the *New York Times* and find the interactive map: https://www.nytimes.com/interactive /2016/04/29/upshot/money-race-and-success-how-your-school -district-compares.html.*

Where does your school district rate? What about those around you? How do race and class either expand or narrow the education opportunities in your community?

Disparities also get baked into available job opportunities based on race and ethnicity. For far too long, the worst industrial and manufacturing jobs were the only jobs open to non-White workers. Earl Fields, who spent nearly forty years working at the Bethlehem Steel Sparrows Point plant said, "See, they had two jobs down there: white jobs and black jobs." According to Fields, those were "the worst jobs, the dirtiest jobs, the nastiest jobs, you name it. In other words, they were black jobs."[5]

For most of the twentieth century, White corporate leaders, educators, and politicians steered Black and immigrant men

---

* If for any reason you cannot access this map, do an internet search for a similar map in your area or search "Money, Race, and Success: How Your School District Compares." (Motoko Rich, Amanda Cox, and Matthew Bloch, "Money, Race, and Success: How Your School District Compares," *New York Times*, April 29, 2016.)

and women into narrowed job opportunities in fields like agriculture, domestic work, service industry, or custodial work. The best-paying jobs, the office jobs, were reserved for White people.

While this has changed over the last fifty years, the impact of decades, and even centuries, of narrow economic opportunities shows up in the vast wealth gap between Black, Brown, and White communities in this nation, especially when there's a cycle that ties educational and economic opportunity to one's economic status as a child. Recent studies on economic mobility demonstrate that where we grow up either expands or narrows our chances to make it economically.

Activation Assignment

Take a look at this interactive map from the *New York Times*: https://www.nytimes.com/interactive/2015/05/03/upshot/the-best-and-worst-places-to-grow-up-how-your-area-compares.html.*

Look at your county and your surrounding counties. How does place expand or narrow opportunity in your region? How do race and ethnicity intersect with opportunity?

Systemic Racism Minimizes Voice

In a democracy, the primary way to voice one's views and preferences is at the ballot box. To minimize voice, take away the vote.

One of the foundational pillars marking the end of slavery was the Fifteenth Amendment, which protects the right to vote. But despite this amendment, the right to vote has always been a struggle in the United States, particularly if you are Black.

---

* If for any reason you cannot access this map, do an internet search for a similar map in your area or search "The Best and Worst Places to Grow Up: How Your Area Compares." (Gregor Aisch, Eric Buth, Matthew Bloch, Amanda Cox, and Kevin Quealy, "The Best and Worst Places to Grow Up: How Your Area Compares," *New York Times*, May 4, 2015.)

For a brief time after the Civil War, Black men could vote, but soon those in power erected new barriers to limit the voting rights of Black citizens without explicitly naming race. This included an understanding clause, whereby workers at local boards of election were able to ask questions of potential voters and were given full authority to determine whether the answers given were correct. They could deny any person the right to register and often did so if the person was Black.

There was also the poll tax. These were statutes, particularly in the South, where people had to pay to vote. The amount could range from one dollar to two dollars per year. In Alabama, for instance, the poll taxes were cumulative, meaning if you registered to vote at age fifty-five but hadn't voted before, you would have to pay a tax for every year you did not vote since the age of twenty-one, meaning the fee would be over thirty dollars just to vote. If one owed $30 in 1940, it would be the equivalent of over $600 in 2020! In essence, this could prevent Black sharecroppers, who often didn't vote because other schemes prevented them, from voting at all.

Women like Fannie Lou Hamer took on these regulations designed to minimize Black voices. During the summer of 1964, Hamer joined others in Mississippi to launch the Mississippi Freedom Democratic Primary, which challenged the state's all-White primary. A White primary in a state that at the time always elected Democrats in general elections meant that if you kept Black people from the primary, their votes in the general election wouldn't matter. The National Democratic Party had already decided that every primary must allow Black people to participate, but they could not in Mississippi. In 1964 in Atlantic City, Hamer went before the rules committee of the Democratic Party and the nation and testified about the terror and violence she and her family had suffered simply for trying to register to vote.

Months later, in March 1965, when Alabama state troopers attacked and beat John Lewis and hundreds of others marching on the Edmund Pettus Bridge in Selma, Alabama, for the right to vote, the nation and President Lyndon Johnson responded. Less than five months later, in early August 1965, Johnson signed the Voting Rights Act, opening the vote to Black men and women across the nation.

But attempts to minimize the voices of the Black, Brown, and Indigenous citizens of this nation have not stopped. Practices like gerrymandering, drawing illogical and even absurd lines to shape statehouse and federal congressional districts, often have the effect of minimizing the voice and influence of Black and Brown citizens. Both major political parties have practiced gerrymandering and continue to do so to tip the scales in their favor, and the ones who tend to pay the price are the non-White populations.

Even in the twenty-first century, some parts of the country continue to pass laws that make voting more difficult. Front and center of our current crisis is this: the gap in political participation between White communities and non-White communities. In the 2020 general election, nearly 71 percent of eligible White voters cast ballots, compared to just over 58 percent of non-White voters. Shouldn't this nearly 13 percent gap be a national embarrassment? To be clear, the reasons are varied, from systemic barriers to those who have given up on their vote mattering at all due to political corruption and ineffectiveness. No matter what side of the aisle or what party or political philosophy one embraces, non-White voters' voices are minimized when the participation gap is so wide.

This, we believe, is an opportunity for us to live undivided. It's a chance for us to come together and find solutions that transcend party lines and are rooted in the dignity of every person and the belief that our country is stronger when more citizens are involved in the processes of democracy.

Some ways to close this gap include making voting more accessible, making voter registration automatic for all citizens, making it easier to vote safely and securely, and upping the percentage of Black and Brown voters. We can work together to root out corruption and inefficiencies so all voters believe and know their votes and their voices matter.

The opportunity to vote is critical to upholding our shared value that we are all created in the image of God. Because we are image bearers, our voices should and must matter.

Another way of minimizing voice is by selecting whose stories and history get told and whose do not. In the winter of 2023, Florida governor Ron DeSantis instructed the state's Department of Education to no longer allow an Advanced Placement African American history course in public high schools. He argued that the course curriculum, which will be available nationwide, promotes indoctrination into a political worldview rather than education. Specifically, he and his supporters claimed the course includes criticism of capitalism and suggests racial discrimination continues today for BIPOC people. The ruling met with strong criticism, particularly from Black students and leaders in Florida, who claimed yet again their voices and story were being minimized and even erased through this decision.

The battle over our history will come and go, but as Michelle Alexander states in her book *The New Jim Crow*, "Any candid observer of American racial history must acknowledge that racism is highly adaptable."[6] Slavery morphed into Jim Crow segregation, which turned into the era of racialized mass incarceration. There will be other battles around who gets to tell the story of our history and how it gets told. What is often true, however, is that the rationale for many of these fights is the protection of the innocence of White children.

While South Africa has had some rocky times since the end of apartheid, one thing they did right was have a truth and reconciliation movement, where the people affected by the evil of apartheid shared their stories. They lifted their voices. The nation listened.

Germany and Rwanda are other examples of countries that are honestly attempting to face their racial history. They did not minimize the voice of the oppressed. To this day, Germany educates their children on what happened during WWII and how, as a country, they are committed to never forget the Holocaust, acknowledging their role in history. Rwanda set a global example in terms of how to heal a country after genocide through their truth and reconciliation process that made it possible for Hutus and Tutsis to attempt to reunify as one nation.

When we minimize history, we minimize voice. We silence the most vulnerable. We forget those we have wronged. We fail to remember and honor the titans. Whether voices are limited by restricting voting or Whitewashing history, stagnancy is exacerbated, contributing to toxicity in our culture and society that almost always harms the most vulnerable among us.

A salient example of this is the Flint water crisis.

A Case Study: A Short Story of Flint, Michigan

How could a city with one of the largest car manufacturers in the world for the better part of the twentieth century deliver poisoned water to its residents just a few decades later? The answer is, in part, that for over one hundred years, Flint, Michigan, restricted movement, narrowed opportunity, and limited the voices of its Black residents. From April 2014 to October

2015, the people of Flint, a Black-majority city, depended on toxic water to bathe, wash dishes, feed their babies, and drink.

For nearly seventy years, Black people fleeing the South to escape legalized segregation and violence came north to places like Flint, seeking good jobs and greater liberty. When they got to Flint, however, the housing opportunities were sparse and restricted. There were only two neighborhoods where Black people could freely live: St. John and Floral Park. Both were redlined, neglected by the city, and highly polluted. When it was time to build new interstate highways and pursue urban renewal, the government designated Floral Park and St. John for demolition, which took nearly a decade, during which time property values fell even further. Over time, Black families moved into other neighborhoods, often through blockbusting, and in the late twentieth century, Flint became a Black-majority city while the suburbs remained overwhelmingly White. Even today a mix of economics and race makes Flint and the surrounding Genesee County highly segregated, with movement of Black and Brown people restricted.

Once Black people arrived in Flint, they faced narrowed education and employment opportunities. The school system—while one of the best in the nation and a model for the community-schools approach, where school buildings served as community centers seven days a week—rested in rigid segregation. Districts were even redrawn during an academic year, something that would be unheard of today, to maintain White-only schools.

In the 1970s, as neighborhoods in parts of the city opened to Black residents, the schools became more diverse and integrated. The number of Black students in Flint city schools rose, while the number of White students plummeted. In 1977, amid this demographic change, the Mott Foundation made a critical decision. After supplementing Flint city schools with anywhere between $1.5 million and nearly $5 million a year since 1935, the foundation decided to end its support. Their rationale? "If a program is assisted by a foundation long enough for its constituents to determine its value to them, the program should in most cases pass to them for on-going funding."[7] What did this mean? It meant that while White families of past decades had received the additional assistance from the Mott Foundation, the now-growing number of Black families would have to bear the burden of bridging the gap that Mott's disinvestment created.

When arguments over government assistance emerge, the stereotype is of Black people gaming the system. Black mothers get labeled "welfare queens." But in Flint, the real disinvestment accelerated as the Black population grew and the White population shrank.

Black residents faced limited economic opportunities as well. At General Motors, which employed as many as eighty thousand people in the Flint region, the only jobs available to Black workers for several decades were the worst ones: janitorial and foundry jobs. Foundry work involved shaping metals and required laboring under intense heat in unhealthy conditions.

More recently, as Flint faced increasing financial challenges, the Michigan state government minimized the voices of Flint residents. While Flint was shrinking and transitioning from a White-majority city to a Black-majority city, the state began to cut the amount of money that would support local governments, shifting more of the burden to local taxes and a shrinking tax base.

The city traditionally had low tax rates, which meant that even during boom times, the local budget could be tight. But as the number of vacant homes rose and incomes fell, the loss of state dollars led to large budget deficits for the city. Between 2002 and 2014, the loss of state dollars to Flint alone totaled $55 million, which would have been more than enough to close annual budget deficits, pay off all city debt, and run a small surplus. Instead, the city struggled to make ends meet. The foreclosure crisis that hit in 2008 further devastated the city and the tax base.

In response to this financial crisis, state law allowed the state to impose an emergency manager on Flint. This unelected appointee, who was not directly accountable to the people of Flint, had the power to make drastic spending cuts to balance the books, including slashing pensions and benefits for city workers. Imposing a city manager meant that local elected officials, including the city council and mayor, had no actual power over decisions.

In essence, Flint was no longer a democracy. The Michigan emergency management system has had deep racial implications for Flint and the entire state. By 2017, over 50 percent of Black people in the state had lived under an emergency manager, compared to only 2 percent of White people. Let that sink in. The pattern was the same in each case: a city that had lost its population and tax base and transitioned from a White to a Black majority would find it nearly impossible to fund local infrastructure just as the state systemically cut support—like the nonprofit Mott Foundation did for Flint schools in 1977.

It was in spring 2014, under this emergency manager, that Flint made the decision to switch from excellent water that came from Lake Huron to highly corrosive water from the Flint River. Slowly, as water sat in pipes made for a city with twice the population, lead began to leak from the pipes and into the water. Then people started getting sick. Residents complained of hair loss, digestive issues, skin irritation, and burning eyes. The impact was not the same everywhere, however.

When water sits stagnant in corroding pipes, the lead and toxins in the water grow. Stagnant water is more dangerous than flowing water. In poorer neighborhoods, with more abandoned homes and vacant lots, water sat stagnant in the pipes for a longer time, giving lead more time to seep into the water. These neighborhoods tended to be Black and Brown communities, while wealthier, Whiter, and more densely populated neighborhoods did not notice as much of a difference, though their water was still unsafe. These conditions lasted for more than eighteen months as local, state, and federal officials pretended nothing was wrong, blamed the residents for the problems, and engaged in cover-ups. In the end, thousands of vulnerable children, toddlers, and babies ingested lead through drinking water that government officials had deemed "safe." The impact of lead poisoning is deep and long-lasting—including hearing and speech issues, slowed growth, and brain damage—and children are especially vulnerable. Systemic racism, over time, coupled with racist neglect, devastated the city of Flint.

Flint is not alone. Throughout the nation, cities have changed. White people have fled to the suburbs. Black and Brown people have been left behind. The tax base in these cities has eroded. The investment in schools has declined. White opportunities have expanded, while Black and Brown families have faced circumstances that must have felt all too familiar. In 1945, Carl Crow of Buick said that the United States consisted of one thousand Flints.[8] While Crow meant to convey the booming economic opportunity that Flint promised, Crow's words ring true for our nation today—we are a nation of a thousand Flints.

We could tell similar stories of restricted movement, narrowed opportunities, and limited voice imposed on Black,

Brown, and Indigenous communities around the nation. This system, over time, reinforces stagnant lives and stagnant communities, where conditions on the ground undoubtedly bring tears to God's eyes, just as Jesus wept over Jerusalem.

Maybe there are answers for Flint that do not focus on racial disparities, but our history suggests that episodes like the Flint water crisis almost always happen in BIPOC communities. We can try to explain away many of these examples, but we just do not see consistent examples of White communities experiencing what happened in Flint. Again and again, it's those who are not White who have a story to tell. This doesn't mean any of us should feel guilty about having safe and clean water, but it should motivate us to work for the same resources for all.

In the late summer of 2022, another water crisis struck a majority-Black town in the United States: Jackson, Mississippi, when filthy and toxic water flowing from taps in the city garnered national news. The issues with the water were not new to Jackson residents, however. We connected with Chevon Chatman of Working Together Jackson during the crisis. In our conversation, she shared that her thirteen-year-old asked, "Is it really a crisis when it's going on all the time?"

Doing justice demands sitting with these disparities that break God's heart—like the ones in Jackson and Flint—and recognizing that while some individuals may have made racist choices along the way, we all tolerate systems that disproportionately hurt our Black and Brown kindred. Let's not forget the effects of this neglect and these racist structures on White people. Think about Flint's water and the 30 percent of the city's White residents. They had poisoned water just as the Black residents did. Yes, you heard that right—systemic racism, while targeting and disproportionately affecting Black and Brown people, can hurt White people too.

When toxicity hits, whether it affects Black or Brown or White, we tend to treat the symptoms. In Flint, instead of going upstream for clean water, city leaders responded by handing out bottled water and free water filters. But they are still struggling to address the systemic problem of lead-based pipes.

If we are to systematically "fix the pipes," moving past stagnancy and the toxicity it breeds toward a flow of racial healing and justice, a realization is required that reckons with where our country is, where it's going, and what our roles are in both.

Yes, it will require a walk of humility to get to an honest realization, and we may experience some painful epiphanies along the way—casualties of the fight for racial healing and solidarity. But when we walk humbly with God, God meets us. When God's power meets the people's willingness to act, incredible change is possible. These opportunities are strengthened by two empowering commitments we must make, which we will explore in the next chapter.

5 Two Empowering Commitments

After reflecting on the roots of our shared story of racism and realizing the deep impact it continues to have, we may be tempted to ask ourselves a logical question regarding the fight against racism: Should we just give up?

Remember we talked about Nehemiah having a choice how he would respond after realizing the state of Jerusalem and its people? You have a choice too.

What will you do about the trouble we're in?

It's not like this is new trouble. Ethnic division and prejudice are as old as humanity. Pharaoh in Egypt weaponized ethnic prejudice by enslaving the Hebrew people and ultimately ordering the genocide of all male Hebrew babies. Later, Moses's own siblings looked askance on his choice to marry Zipporah, who was Cushite (translation: of African descent).

During Jesus's life, it was common to assign different values to people based on their ethnicity. If you were a foreigner, woman, or child, you were viewed and treated as property owned by the local rulers or male head of the household. Samaritans faced intense prejudice as well, something that shows up again and again in the Gospels.

You might be thinking, *Is there really anything I can do to make a difference when it comes to a problem that's been around—literally—forever?*

We want to "coach you up" in this chapter, first by empathizing with the real struggle we all feel when it comes to living undivided. Then, we want to give you a dose of encouragement as we turn the corner toward how we can create a better story and lasting change. It starts with two empowering commitments—resisting weariness and rejecting powerlessness.

Resisting Weariness

One of our friends in this work once made a statement that immediately became "sticky" in our brains. He had spent the better part of a year talking with Christian leaders about how they were addressing racism and injustice in their contexts. While he was encouraged by some of the stories, his honest assessment was that a majority of Christian leaders felt they "can't win, they CAN lose, and they can't quit" when it comes to addressing racism and injustice. What a bummer!

Perhaps you're as discouraged by that as we were the first time we heard it. But doesn't it also ring true? Do you feel like we live in a culture where one poorly placed word or phrase can make you susceptible to judgment and worse? Can you imagine being marginalized by simply offering your personal perspective? We've got to be honest about the real temptation to grow weary in the journey of living undivided, regardless of our racial or ethnic background. Many Black, Indigenous, and other People of Color reading this book feel exhausted right now. You picked up this book hoping to hear something that sounds like a fresh approach or a viable path forward. For People of Color, the struggle to end racism isn't optional—it's a matter of survival.

Some People of Color reading this book have been on the receiving end of hate, judgment, fear, and discrimination. You have been mistreated and abused. Maybe you've fought back. You've joined, started, or led an organization. You've been a trailblazer in your field. You've spoken out. You may have even participated in marches and protests. But now you're wondering if it's worth the effort. In dark moments, you sometimes think there's nothing you can do to change anything.

Others have chosen to exit predominantly White spaces, including predominantly White churches. Why? Because, sadly, many predominantly White spaces and the people who lead them continue to have cultures that are oppressive, exploitative, and/or harmful to BIPOC leaders.

For many White brothers and sisters reading this book, you may be weary of continually hearing that you're responsible for racism that occurred before you were even born. You've felt crushing waves of guilt and shame as you've heard lectures about your inherent privileges. Perhaps it feels like everywhere you turn—especially on social media—you're being labeled a White supremacist and a bigot. You feel like when it comes to race, you simply can't win—you're in a box you can never get out of. You suspect that even if you did do something to challenge racism, it wouldn't be enough to matter.

Other White people may feel like you've taken important steps to address racism in your life. You've done soul-searching work, recognized ways you may have been complicit, and built friendships across race and ethnicity at work, in your church, or in your neighborhood. You've made a lot of progress, but the task of making broader change has you . . . well, just plain tired.

We believe God wants to meet our weariness with an empowering word! Galatians 6:9 says, "So let us not grow weary in doing what is right, for we will reap at harvest time, if we do not give up." God is birthing a fresh movement toward racial healing and justice, but just like the act of childbirth, new life does not emerge without pain. Yet God's promise through Galatians 6:9 is powerful and simply stated: *you be faithful, and I will be fruitful.* This is God's encouragement to us as we do the difficult and painful work involved in living undivided—that our faithfulness and commitment to a flow of healing and justice that repairs wounds and cultivates equitable systems where all people flourish *will produce good outcomes.* To see it, we must commit ourselves to resisting the temptation to grow weary.

The Price of Weariness

We know many of you are more than a little weary of the conversation about race. Giving in to weariness comes at a far greater cost than you might expect.

What concerns us is that far too many of our exhausted kindred are leaving the church and are in danger of leaving Jesus as well. We have both grieved moments where, after growing convicted of their own racism and the racism that marks the church, some of our White brothers and sisters have chosen to leave the church rather than do the work of repentance and reconciliation. We have also been heartbroken when, after growing disillusioned and embittered by the church's role (or lack thereof) in the fight against racism, People of Color have left the church.

Hear us: congregations gathering in the name of Jesus are called to persist in this work.

God's heart is not for his people to give up on this joint project of racial healing and justice but that they stay in the game. In the early 1970s, Albert Hirschman, a Jewish-German economist, wrote an important book called *Exit, Voice, and Loyalty.* The premise is that consumers in a marketplace of ever-expanding options are increasingly leaving behind organizations that don't meet all their expectations.[1] Let's be real—this is especially true for churches today. People can choose to exit one church for a church down the block whenever the congregation fails to live up to their expectations on any number of fronts, from the quality of the music to the strength of the children's ministry to theological positions.

When met with a dilemma, more and more people are choosing to exit, and often the decision to leave one congregation results in leaving the church altogether. There is another possibility. They can instead choose to stay, remain committed, and work with others to ensure their voice is not only critiquing but also shaping the direction of the organization.

We see far too many exiting the church right now, and with good reason. We simply ask you to go before God and ask whether he may be calling you to instead bring your voice to the church. No church is perfect, and (ahem) neither are you. But every church is made stronger when those with differing points of view choose not to exit from relationship but to engage from a place of continual humility and curiosity. If we're to move beyond stagnancy as a church, we who are committed to racial healing, solidarity, and justice must stay in the game. We get to choose voice over exit. In partnership with the Holy Spirit, we can resist weariness.

Rejecting Powerlessness

We are both avid sports fans, with a particular loyalty to the Cincinnati Bengals. It has been enjoyable to see our beloved football team grow in relevance and respect around the National Football League. A big reason for this is that the team is now playing to win instead of playing not to lose. They've rejected the narrative that has hung like a cloud over the franchise for many years—that the Cincinnati "Bungles" would find a way to lose every time. Things start to change when a franchise, a church, a family, or a person rejects the illusion of powerlessness.

In a far different sense, I (Chuck) am familiar with the tension between playing to win and playing not to lose. A few years ago, I went on an adventure that pushed me to my physical, mental, and spiritual limits. At the time, I was a motorcycle rider and had recently made the switch from your typical street riding to off-road riding. My friend and senior pastor at Crossroads, Brian Tome, has been an avid off-road motorcyclist for years. Brian led a group of novice off-road riders (me being one of them) on an epic motorcycle ride through the Colorado Backcountry Discovery Route. The ride included aggressive terrain and harrowing mountainside passes at twelve thousand feet of elevation.

As someone who was both new to this kind of riding and scared of heights (remember my Apple Watch incident on the bridge?), the trip was the most intense physical challenge I've ever experienced. To top it off, a film crew recorded the entire trip, which became a spiritual reality show titled *Phantom Lake*. Playing not to lose would have led me to say "no thank you" to this adventure. Playing to win had me believing I could learn, grow, and succeed in doing something that made me quake in my boots.

The trip was a bonding experience with Brian and the other riders, and it was going quite well for me . . . that is, until the last day of the trip. The show was called *Phantom Lake* because that was the name of our destination: a nearly inaccessible lake on a mountaintop. The only path to the lake included river crossings, riding over rocks, and more aggressive maneuvering than I'd ever had to pull off in all my years of riding motorcycles. Things were looking up, and so was I, when all of a sudden I took a hard fall on the bike and couldn't feel my left foot. When the feeling came back a second later, it was the most searing pain you could imagine. I screamed out in pain, and the rest of the riders quickly got off their bikes and ran to me. They heard me because we were connected through wireless headsets. Because we were filming the whole thing for a limited series on a major streaming service, the camera crew, which included an EMT, also ran to my location.

After peeling off some of my riding gear and my boots, it was very clear that I had broken some bones—more specifically, three bones in my left foot. The team laid hands on me and prayed, then I was taken off the mountain and driven to the closest emergency room, which was two hours away in Wyoming. The trip was over for me, but my fall, my injury, and my reaction will now live in infamy! After nine days of challenge and growth, of overcoming fear and my limits as a new rider, my chance to make it to Phantom Lake was cut off at the knees. It was a painful way to end what otherwise was an incredible experience.

Rejecting powerlessness means facing our fears and recognizing we are capable of far more than we could have imagined, especially together. This doesn't mean we will be free of challenges, bumps, bruises, and yes, even a few broken bones along the way. We will still have seasons of struggle, and we will be failing forward.

My next trip out West was in 2021 when I took my son on a father-son adventure in Montana—a trip that had been in the works for almost a year. We went with a group of amazing dads and sons, and all the boys were between the ages of twelve and fourteen, so this was supposed to be a kind of rite-of-passage-to-manhood experience for them.

As you may recall, I was born and raised a city kid on the streets of Philadelphia. While I love the outdoors now, that wasn't always the case. Remember, though, the last time I went out West, I came home with a significant injury. As you might imagine, as I was flying to Montana, I had moments when I thought, *Last time I did something like this, it didn't end well. But lightning doesn't strike twice, right?*

My son and I landed in Montana, and it was breathtakingly beautiful. During our first hours there, great connections were already beginning to be made among the group—and especially between my son and me. This was going to be a trip to remember.

The next day we went on a low-key hike that ended at a fun watering hole where the dads and sons swam in a freshwater creek. But I never quite reached my destination. Why? Well, about five minutes from the creek, we were hiking along a cliffside about fifteen feet above the ground when, in an instant, the ground gave way underneath me. I went tumbling down the cliff and landed hard at the bottom . . . and I had broken something *again*. (Aside: I'm tired of going out West with friends and needing them to put their hands on me to pray over an injury!)

As I sat on the creek bank, I was tempted to embrace self-pity and quit. Thankfully, the men with me gave me a place to feel, process, and ultimately realize that while the trip was going to look different than I'd anticipated, that fall and injury didn't have to rob my son and me of an opportunity to bond and have an adventure together.

It turned out that I'd fractured my elbow, which meant doing the rest of the week in a sling. But I stayed, and my son and I had an incredible experience we'll never forget.

Why are we sharing these mishaps with you? Because when it comes to racial healing and justice, regardless of your racial background, you can feel like it's a losing proposition. You can feel like the next fall, the next mistake, the next challenge is right around the corner. You can feel completely powerless and want to give up.

What Hangs in the Balance?

Given the gravity and intensity of the racial divide and the perpetual presence of racial injustice, have you had moments of anger, frustration, or sheer helplessness? Moments where you've asked yourself, *What makes me think I can make a difference? How in the world will this ever change?* We've certainly asked those questions of ourselves.

But what if these aren't the right questions to ask? What if there are better questions, like *What hangs in the balance if I don't try to make a difference? What becomes possible if I reject powerlessness and try?*

Throwing up our hands in defeat has a real cost. Giving in to powerlessness has a price. Imagine giving up on being a parent. If you have children like we do, that may sound insane, and yet there are times throughout parenthood when children make choices that are outside our control, especially as they get older, and we can easily give up hope and stop engaging altogether.

If you give up on a house mid-renovation, it doesn't get finished. If you give up on your work, you don't get paid. If you give up on your relationship with your spouse, it falls apart. Anytime you allow the illusion of powerlessness to cause you to stop trying, there's a cost, and there's the loss of a benefit that only you can uniquely offer to the situation.

Let's be clear. There's a deep cost to avoidance, and that cost builds over time. The result is stagnancy, and the repercussions are devastating.

What Gets in Your Way?

If we can all become aware of what our own tendencies are in our fight against injustice, we'll be far less likely to grow weary and get stuck. In LivingUNDIVIDED, we spend time orienting people to the common ways conversations on race get derailed. We call these stagnancy drivers, because they are the places where the "flow" of racial healing and justice can devolve into stagnant waters of disagreement, discouragement, or greater divisiveness.

Have any of the following gotten in the way of your journey toward living undivided?

Flight. This is when we bail on the work and flee relationships and efforts that are vital to bringing healing and justice. It's easy for tensions to rise, causing us to back away to create healthy space to process our thoughts and feelings. But we must always be willing to come back to the table, again and again.

There was a two-year period when I (Chuck) all but abandoned the work of racial healing and justice. I was tired of the struggle and what it required of me as a leader in predominantly White spaces, so I began to distract myself with different "good Christian activities" while leaving others to have the hard and necessary conversations about race.

My passivity was costly, as it shifted the burden of the work unfairly onto others who thought they could count on me as a colaborer. What I should have done was been honest with them about my struggle and then worked alongside them to determine what rest and recovery could look like for me so that I wasn't leaving them high and dry.

Fix. We want to find the quickest and easiest solution and solve racism in a single bound. The odyssey of fighting racism requires perseverance and commitment.

Early in my (Troy's) pastoral career, my church hired a Black staff member who joined an otherwise all-White staff and largely White congregation. Over the next few years, during this person's tenure, tensions emerged. Instead of encouraging and challenging people to work through these tensions in healthy ways, I continuously elected to go into fix-it mode.

To protect the Black staff member, I'd try to manage and tamp down issues, which inhibited our congregation. I also did no favors for the staff person, who was more than capable of engaging these challenges directly had I not paternalistically gone into fix-it mode.

Fake. Instead of confronting your trauma and the pain that's resulted from racism, you pretend everything's okay.

There have been many times when I (Chuck) have been the only Person of Color in the room and something harmful was said or a decision was made that centered on Whiteness. At times I default to a "go along to get along" mindset, remaining quiet or laughing off the inappropriate comment just to be seen as a good team player. The thing is, these moments are never without consequences for me. They leave me feeling ashamed at the betrayal of my own values, which over time diminishes my sense of agency and undermines my integrity.

Freeze. We are afraid to say or do the wrong thing. We protect ourselves by choosing silence and inaction.

I (Troy) easily enter the freeze mindset in new multiracial environments when the topic of race comes up. I don't know very many people in the room and they don't know me, and I tend to freeze up. I don't want to make a mistake, especially when these people don't know anything about me.

So I tend to listen and wait. I tell myself I'm simply making space for Black and Brown and other People of Color to share, but what I'm really doing is shrinking and hiding. This gets in the way of my growth and also places the burden of carrying the conversation and demonstrating vulnerability entirely on People of Color in the room while I'm a mere observer.

Fight. We can get to a place where our desire isn't reconciliation and we are instead trying to get an enemy to surrender and retreat.

> Be angry but do not sin; do not let the sun go down on your anger, and do not make room for the devil. (Eph. 4:26–27)

There have been times when my (Chuck's) efforts to right racial wrongs have been motivated by anger alone. Anger is a powerful emotion, and an appropriate one—especially when you, someone you love, or even someone with whom you identify has been wronged. Part of my journey has included learning how to express anger in healthy ways rooted in love, especially when I'm a victim of racial discrimination, without letting the anger fester.

It's important for me to acknowledge and address the legitimate hurt behind my anger. "Stuffing" my feelings related to these wounds and offenses has sometimes caused me to blow up at people who are on the opposite side of an issue as if they are my mortal enemy. I've had shouting matches and I've written off people whom I now see God may have placed in my life to bring more diversity, depth, and breadth to my understanding of what my call to racial healing, solidarity, and justice demands. Taking time to acknowledge my hurt and approaching these relationships without the need to be right has helped me grow in my ability to listen, learn, and lead well.

Fold. The struggle for justice is overwhelming and long, and over time, it's easy to believe nothing can change.

When I (Troy) focus too much on my Twitter feed, the cable news, and angst-filled conversations, I get really discouraged. Sometimes it feels like we're fated to struggle with racism, and things are only getting worse.

I'm not much of a poker player, but I know enough that one of the choices card players make is simply to fold—toss in their cards and give up. I sometimes have this temptation when it comes to race.

There have been a few times when I put too much hope in the outcome of a particular election, and even when it turned out as I'd wanted it to, racism in this nation and the church seemed to get worse (and we can probably say this no matter what party or candidate has won recently). When I believe the lie that racism is part of our fate and the cause is hopeless, I fold, which does nothing to further what I'm fighting for.

To fold is the ultimate precursor to stagnancy.

Just like we do with powerlessness and weariness, we have to overcome our tendency toward stagnancy. There's so much work to be done. There's so much work *already* being done. Together, you and I have irreplaceable roles to play in the story God is writing in reconciling God's children.

Take a moment and prayerfully review the list above. Which of these is a challenge you're presently wrestling with? Invite God to bring his power, love, and strength to help you overcome whatever is getting in the way. You matter to God, and you matter to the work of racial healing and justice. We're praying with you at this moment, and we're confident that whatever is in the way will be rendered powerless by the grace and presence of God's Spirit in your life. We're also confident that as it says in Philippians 1:6, "The one who began a good work in you will continue to complete it until the day of Jesus Christ." When we resist weariness and reject powerlessness, we get a front-row seat to God's good work among us as we pursue a life undivided.

Is This a Church Thing?

We were hosting an UNDIVIDED experience for a cohort of public leaders in a city near Dayton, Ohio. Even though not everyone in the group was a Christian, they decided to do our Jesus-rooted content as a way of bringing city leaders together to help advance the work of racial healing and justice in their community.

Every week includes a faith grounding—a teaching from Scripture that undergirds the discussion on how to bring about racial unity. On a week that was particularly Scripture heavy, a participant paused after one of the faith groundings and said, "Wait, is this a church thing?"

Her name is Karina, and I (Chuck) was in the room when she asked this question. A pregnant silence fell over the group. And what Karina said next gave me the chills (the good kind). She said, "I left church because they weren't talking about injustice, and if you're telling me there's a church that's willing to talk about this, then I feel like God is calling me back to church."

During a time when many congregations are struggling in the wake of the pandemic, Crossroads and my (Troy's) church are growing. Sanctuary Church is a multiracial congregation in Columbus led by a Black pastor, and it continually makes the decision not to be stagnant when it comes to race. Pastor Rich Johnson and other preachers continually bring the truth of God's Word and Jesus's love to the racial tensions and injustices that mark so much of our culture. By proactively engaging, the church offers a credible witness to a world looking for courageous leadership on race.

We can think that our silence or stagnancy isn't hurting anyone. We can let our fear of doing or saying the wrong thing keep us from doing something. But we should remember that there are many people like Karina who may have given up on the church but haven't given up on God. And many of them are waiting for followers of Jesus to resist weariness and reject powerlessness to do the work of loving courageously for racial healing and justice with a distinctly Jesus-style approach.

If you find yourself in a state of stagnancy, you don't have to stay that way. In fact, God desires the opposite—God desires a flow of racial healing and justice that draws you closer to your Creator.

Walking humbly requires at least two steps:

1. *Being rooted.* This means recognizing our identity as a citizen in the family of God, as a person created in God's image. *That* is who we are at our core. When we begin to see ourselves through this eternal lens, we can also see our brothers and sisters more clearly. We can see their pain. We feel it *with* them, because we are rooted in it together.

2. *A realization.* While the work of racial healing and justice is not without difficulty, it's also a place where we can experience deep and lasting joy and growth as followers of Jesus. The realization we have come to believe about living undivided is that we don't have to do this . . . we *get* to do this! Walking humbly in this work, though, requires a continual realization that, as a friend in ministry, Pastor Karl Martin says, "we are the project." The most significant change needed to live undivided is the change that God wants to bring about in our hearts.

Some of these steps may come at a price. Humility is rarely painless. But it's *always* worth it.

EXAMINE YOUR STORY

1. In what ways have you been playing not to lose when it comes to race? If you lead an organization, in what ways has your organization been playing not to lose?

2. What's God saying to you about how you can continue to resist weariness and reject powerlessness? What's your first step?

3. Reflect on Philippians 1:6 again: "I am confident of this, that the one who began a good work in you will continue to complete it until the day of Jesus Christ." Ask God to reveal/continue to reveal the good work you are called to do for racial healing and justice. Then ask him for the courage to humbly respond to this invitation.

PART 3

RESPOND

LOVE MERCY

3. RESPOND—Prioritizing relationships with the people most affected by injustice and people with different experiences and perspectives regarding race and ethnicity.

4. RECKON

Through the prophecy of Micah, God also said what is good *and* required is to *love mercy*.

We don't use the word *mercy* often in our everyday vernacular. If I were to ask you what it meant, you'd probably connect mercy to some level of radical forgiveness. Yes, having a forgiving heart is merciful. But mercy itself is a bit more nuanced.

The New Revised Standard Version Updated Edition words Micah 6:8 a little differently. "To love mercy" becomes "to love kindness." When someone loves kindness, they're kind. When someone loves kindness, they're empathetic. When someone loves kindness, they're compassionate. Mercy has an emotive connotation that isn't summed up with the act of forgiveness. Mercy takes a step *toward* someone. To hear them and to know them.

Remember that the UNDIVIDED Circle isn't linear. We're not suggesting you have to first master walking humbly through the steps of root and realize before deciding to love mercy. But understand that the entire process *must* be framed in love.

How is this love defined? Greg Boyd, a pastor in Minneapolis, shared in a sermon the best definition we've heard for Christlike love: *ascribing worth to others, even at cost to yourself* (see 1 John 3:16). Think about it. That's what Jesus did for us, right? He demonstrated our immeasurable value to God as image bearers by paying the ultimate price of death on the cross to restore us to a right relationship with God.

This is a critical part of the UNDIVIDED Circle—to love, which demands relationships, especially across differences.

To love mercy means to intentionally seek out those who are hurting and to be willing to compassionately enter into their pain. But before you can enter into someone's pain, you have to get to know them. And you have to let them know you too.

That's the third step in the UNDIVIDED Circle.

Step Three: Respond

In the month of Nisan, in the twentieth year of King Artaxerxes, when wine was served him, I carried the wine and gave it to the king. Now, I had never been sad in his presence before. (Neh. 2:1)

Those who serve people with great power instinctively know to hide emotion or weakness, and Nehemiah was no different. In fact, Nehemiah said he'd never before shown sadness in front of the king. Think about it—you probably wouldn't want to cry in front of your boss. It's an unnatural posture. Now imagine that your boss is an impossibly powerful king of the Persian nation. Showing any range of emotion would cost a great deal of pride.

Masking emotions is a move of self-preservation and safety that's a common theme in the story of Black, Indigenous, and People of Color in America. In his classic *The Souls of Black*

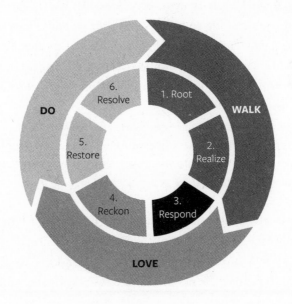

Folk, W. E. B. Du Bois talks about living life behind a veil—being able to see out and observe what's going on in White society but hiding what's going on in one's heart and in the broader Black community. In a sense, Nehemiah, as part of an oppressed people, was living life behind a veil.

Faced with the painful realization that Jerusalem and the people were in trouble, Nehemiah resisted stagnancy by choosing to be vulnerable in front of the king—a move that could have cost him his position, his status, or even his life. Nehemiah's choice was rooted in love—ascribing worth to his disenfranchised Israelite brothers and sisters, at a cost to himself. Nehemiah chose to love mercy—to enter into the pain of those who were hurting.

He took a huge relational risk when he removed the proverbial veil in front of the king, who immediately recognized that Nehemiah was sad. And this next confession by Nehemiah is telling: "Then I was very much afraid" (v. 2).

Yes, it can be terrifying to be vulnerable. It's risky to share your story, including your flaws and your wounds. This courageous act will remove the veil between you and another. Regardless of his fear, Nehemiah found the courage to share not only his emotions but also what was driving his grief—the news of a destroyed Jerusalem.

> Then I said to the king, "If it pleases the king, and if your servant has found favor with you, I ask that you send me to Judah, to the city of my ancestors' graves, so that I may rebuild it." (v. 5)

Notice that Nehemiah mentions not the people of Jerusalem but rather the physical state of the city and the destruction of its gates. Even in sharing part of his heart with the king, Nehemiah wanted to protect the people, who were his primary concern.

Perhaps he didn't want to draw attention to those who weren't in captivity, fearing the king might attempt to finish what the Babylonians had started by having troops round them up and send them into exile as well.

When the king asked what Nehemiah wanted, Nehemiah's first instinct was to pray and then ask boldly for the king to send him back to Jerusalem to rebuild the city. He even went so far as to request safe passage, as well as the necessary building materials to rebuild Jerusalem's walls. Miraculously, Nehemiah said, "The king granted me what I asked, for the gracious hand of my God was upon me" (v. 8).

That very same hand of God is upon you as well.

6 The Power of Community

Loving mercy happens best in community, and community demands that we respond to one another by engaging in meaningful and vulnerable ways. We're writing this book together because in December 2014, we both made decisions to truly relate to one another.

Let's revisit the story of how Chuck and I met through the lens of loving mercy. In 2014, I (Troy) became director of the AMOS Project in Cincinnati and began rebuilding the organization. We went from having a handful of congregations dedicated to the work of racial and economic justice to over forty in only a few years.

About six months into my tenure, I finally got up the courage to reach out to Crossroads Church and their founding pastor, Brian Tome. Why did this take courage? Well, Crossroads wasn't only the largest church in our region; it was larger than any other three churches in the area combined. Suffice it to say, engaging a congregation that averaged nearly thirty thousand people every weekend was intimidating.

The other reason was I knew Brian, and I knew he had little patience for organizations that talked a big game but never did anything. I was prepared when Brian asked, "What has AMOS ever done?" Apparently, my answer was good enough, because Brian suggested I meet with a couple of key staff people, Tim Senff and Chuck Mingo.

I knew Tim already, and that meeting went well. Then, on a cold December morning, I met Chuck in the atrium of Crossroads' anchor campus.

One way to describe the first fifteen minutes of our conversation is that Chuck was wearing his veil. I asked him how he was feeling about Ferguson, the emergence of the Movement for Black Lives, and the growing racial reckoning that 2014 represented in our nation. And Chuck gave the safest, most noncontroversial answers in the history of humankind. Chuck didn't know me, and I needed to build trust.

About thirty minutes into the conversation, as I shared more of my story and described my recent trip to Ferguson, why I went, and what I felt being there, Chuck made the decision to truly relate to me. He lifted the veil a bit and started sharing more deeply and honestly. And in that conversation, we each decided that we'd need each other for the path God was calling us to. I invited Chuck to get more engaged with the work of AMOS, and a few months later, he invited me to be on the design team to build UNDIVIDED. The journey we walk together started with an intentional meeting, curiosity, and vulnerability.

The Power of Responding

Over the past several years, I've learned a great deal from Chuck, who reminds me of the importance of hope, curiosity, earnestness, and courage in the struggle for racial healing, solidarity, and justice. While my days of pastoring a church ended in 2013, Chuck continues to navigate the high call to lead a diverse community well. I can be quick to judge and filled with cynicism, but Chuck is filled with grace and ready to listen and learn. He balances my prophetic edge with a pastor's heart, and one of the greatest blessings of this season in my life is not only becoming Chuck's friend but also following him on this vital mission.

The time-tested and God-approved journey out of stagnancy demands relationships. Without community, we get stuck. Any flow of racial healing and justice that repairs wounds and cultivates equitable systems where all people flourish requires relationships—lots of them, over time and across differences.

A comprehensive picture of the power of responding can't be contained in the pages of this book. However, we want to share a few illustrations to show how responding leads to pivotal experiences that serve as catalysts for change—not just in the lives of those moving through the UNDIVIDED Circle, but for entire families and communities.

Taisha Rojas-Parker

Taisha serves as a facilitator for the UNDIVIDED experiences. Hear her story of the power of community below.

I grew up in Harlem, New York City—Black Harlem. Growing up in a neighborhood that was all Black, my experience was the same as the people around me. I wasn't around different cultures or communities to really be able to compare and contrast my experience as it related to race.

But I always yearned to learn more about different communities and groups of people. Funny story, I went to Xavier University, and when asked why I selected it, I said, "Well, I've never really been around White people before." I was curious. I wanted to know. And my understanding was that to be successful in business and in life, you had to know how to interact with White people. So my approach to race and racism was really very kind of task-oriented, without an understanding of the depths and foundation of racism.

When I moved from New York City to Cincinnati, that's when I really saw the difference between how I was viewed by people who look different from me. I felt my competencies and skills were questioned simply because of how I looked, which was something I had never experienced before. That experience planted seeds of curiosity and questions that I later cultivated through UNDIVIDED.

I was one of the first participants of UNDIVIDED. I was struck by the different experiences those of us who were People of Color had compared to those who were White. I realized that I *had* experienced racism, at least at a systemic level, but I hadn't been aware of it at the time.

Last year I decided to understand not only the system but also how God sees racism and wants us to bridge the gaps between race with love, peace, understanding, and even challenge where appropriate.

Later, when I facilitated an UNDIVIDED experience, my co-host was Elliot. Elliot was someone who looked different from me, but it was great because we were able to leverage each other's strengths. We were able to leverage each other's talents. And we were able to do that in a way that really demonstrated that no matter who you are or what you look like, we all come with skills.

Elliot was strong at structure, framing things, and asking questions. And I was good at creating space for people to process, sit in the discomfort, and work through the feelings of it all. Through our partnership, we were able to have some really strong breakthroughs in our session. It was powerful.

I am so excited to be a part of the UNDIVIDED program, to learn and grow together with cohorts, because we as facilitators learn something new every time we do it. And it continues with the evolution of our hearts and minds and spirits to overcome something that is deeply rooted and extremely systemic—something we need to pluck out as an evil root in our society so we can heal and grow and thrive as a people of God.

Vince Lam

Vince Lam, a Chinese American, is one of our participants and now a staff member with UNDIVIDED. Before the LivingUNDIVIDED experience, Vince wouldn't have qualified himself as a racist. In fact, Vince hadn't yet fully embraced his own racial identity. Being neither Black nor White, Vince was unsure of the role he had to play in America's "Black and White" story of racism.

Fast-forward to Vince experiencing LivingUNDIVIDED, where he sat around a table of people who didn't look like him and discussed the most vulnerable aspects of who he was. Vince's decision to relate beckoned him to look back at the murder of George Floyd, where video showed an Asian American police officer standing off to the side with his hands in his pockets.

Vince said that the visual of that officer brought into sharper focus the problem with racism today in America. "It's not just a White or Black problem to solve. We've been trying that for years. The power for change lies in the hands of the bystanders. Those of us who have discounted ourselves as not having any stake in the fight for racial justice."

Today, Vince continues to expand his leadership and influence of others as a leader in our movement. We're thankful for leaders like Vince and Taisha and many others who are choosing to love mercy through deep and vulnerable relationships.

Chambers

Let's be honest. For some of us, this is more difficult than it sounds, because more and more of us are living in our own echo chambers. An echo chamber is an environment in which a person encounters only beliefs or opinions that coincide with their own, so that their existing views are reinforced and alternative ideas are not considered. If we're not intentional, we tend to surround ourselves with people who look like us, act like us, and think like us. In this era of social media, even the math behind our feeds (the algorithms) can accelerate our division. What we see on social media is another invisible system that can perpetuate distrust and even injustice.

Think about your neighborhood. How racially and ethnically diverse is it? Do the majority of your neighbors look and think like you do? When it comes to election season, do the yard signs in your neighborhood mostly, or exclusively, feature the same candidates and positions?

Reflect on your church. Is your congregation almost entirely made up of your same race or ethnicity? Do the people in your faith community tend to think alike on major social and political issues, or is there diversity?

Consider your online activity. Do your Facebook, Instagram, or Twitter feeds largely reflect an echo chamber, where almost all the perspectives you hear line up with your own? Some of this is natural, but to truly respond as part of the LivingUNDIVIDED journey, we must intentionally break out of these echo chambers.

These questions about our echo chambers aren't meant to lead to shame or judgment. This isn't a pass/fail test; it's simply meant to give you an opportunity to reflect on whom you interact with on a regular basis. What's most important is what you do next. Will you choose to break out of echo chambers and choose courageous love? If you're willing to do this work continually, you will not only experience a richer life but also be further empowered to pursue racial healing and justice in ways that align with the heart of Jesus.

Because not relating comes with great cost. Echo chambers breed stagnation. Remember what we said about the dangers found in stagnant water? About the damage it can cause? Echo chambers are like stagnant ponds that breed and grow disease, distress, division, destruction, and death.

If we're going to get out of our stagnant echo chambers, we have to make the courageous decision to relate across differences. Here are a few actions you can take to bust out of your echo chamber.

First, look up. To do something as countercultural as bridging across differences, we need God's power and perspective. Remember Revelation 7:9? The apostle John saw a vision of heaven, and saw people of every tribe, tongue, and nation. God's future for us does not include echo chambers—and it certainly doesn't include racial and ethnic divisions.

Second, look in. Make sure you're pursuing this important work of bridging with a whole heart. Engaging across differences out of obligation or guilt can lead to more damage for yourself and others. Also, remember the important healing work God is doing in your heart and your life. We encourage you to be courageous in breaking out of your echo chambers, and we also encourage you to make sure these brave spaces are also as safe as possible, particularly for BIPOC people.

Next, look around. While we often assume that we live, work, worship, and play in environments without diversity, once we truly examine our context, we may be surprised by what we find. According to the 2020 census, even rural America is more diverse than it used to be.[1]

Truly examine who lives in your community, who attends your congregation, and who makes up the student body at your child's school. Is there diversity? If so, how might you begin to build relationships across differences? Nothing will move you out of stagnancy faster than an honest and vulnerable relationship with someone who looks different from you.

Looking around also may include not doing this alone. What friends or family or members of your congregation might go on this journey with you?

Finally, if you're still struggling, look again. If your church is made up almost exclusively of one race or ethnicity, is your congregation part of a denomination or a network of churches that includes those with racial and ethnic differences? Is there a congregation across town or in another part of your region with more diversity? Are there connections online that might get you out of your echo chamber?

The important thing is to realize that none of this will happen without intentionality and a little effort on your part. Bridging across differences demands courage, resilience, and endurance. Also, let us caution you to approach these relationships with sensitivity. The intent is to build authentic relationships where "iron sharpens iron" (Prov. 27:17), not to check a box.

Pay attention to power dynamics as well. If you're White and looking to engage across race, think about joining an organization or a congregation with BIPOC leadership. The dominant model of multiracial congregations and organizations has depended on People of Color crossing the divide to join White-led churches, businesses, or organizations. If you're White, this is a chance to interrupt this pattern and submit to and learn from BIPOC leadership.

If you're Black, Indigenous, or a Person of Color, we recognize that crossing racial and ethnic divides may already be part of your daily life. We did an exercise with some of the lead facilitators of our UNDIVIDED experiences where we asked them to reflect on their echo chambers, and one Black leader made an interesting comment. She wondered if she is relating only across race. Her commitment was to find a few places in her life rhythms where she would choose to be with other Black people, as she recognized she needed this space to simply be and freely exhale.

While we don't encourage a total disengagement from other cultures and races, we do recognize that the path of healing and wholeness sometimes demands seasons where we can connect deeply with our own racial or ethnic communities.

As we respond, let's remember that in the end, we need each other. We are created for community.

EXAMINE YOUR STORY

1. Look up. What's your prayer to God as you start this journey?

2. Look in. What are your motivations for building bridges with people from other races and ethnic groups? What ongoing healing do you need to prioritize as you build new cross-racial relationships?

3. Look around. As you consider your relationships where you live, work, worship, and play, what perspectives or experiences are missing? Who might be a bridge builder with you?

4. Look again. Widen the parameters of your search. Pray for surprising and unexpected new connections.

PART 4

RECKON

LOVE MERCY

3. RESPOND

4. RECKON—Charting a new direction through healing, repentance, and transformation.

There's certainly a relational aspect to loving mercy. But there's an action piece as well—an effort to get to the bottom of how the situation came to be as bad as it is. An effort to take stock.

That's the fourth step in the UNDIVIDED Circle.

Step Four: Reckon

Prior to leaving for Jerusalem, Nehemiah began to reckon with his calling by courageously sharing the state of the city of Jerusalem with King Artaxerxes, giving the king the opportunity to reckon with and share responsibility for his part in the utter disarray of his kingdom.

As Dr. Martin Luther King Jr.'s organization, the Southern Christian Leadership Conference, embraced the slogan "To redeem the soul of America," Nehemiah boldly invited the king to redeem the city of Jerusalem, and the king rose to the challenge.

It's time for us to rise to the challenge too.

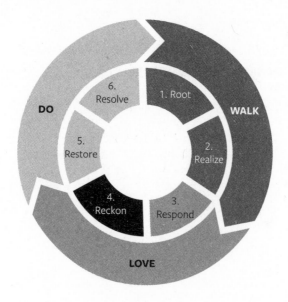

Next, Nehemiah cashed in on his resources and arrived in Jerusalem. He spent three days in the city, and only after those three days did he do a night ride around Jerusalem to inspect the destruction.

So what did Nehemiah do during those first three days? In all probability, he was relating to the people, checking on them, and getting a feel for their pain, their challenges, and their hopes and dreams. He was also familiarizing himself with the people's assets and gifts, which would be critical for the mission that awaited them. Only after several days of connection with the people of Jerusalem was Nehemiah ready to inspect the physical state of the city.

Following the midnight inspection, Nehemiah gathered the people, which he described as "the Jews, the priests, the nobles, the officials, and the rest who were to do the work" (Neh. 2:16). In other words, Nehemiah called a mass community meeting and, having already built some trust over his first few days of relating with them, invited them to reckon with the state of their community:

> Then I said to them, "You see the trouble we are in, how Jerusalem lies in ruins with its gates burned. Come, let us rebuild the wall of Jerusalem, so that we may no longer suffer disgrace."
> (v. 17)

Now, maybe the people of Jerusalem had stopped seeing the trouble they were in before Nehemiah arrived. Maybe they had become stagnant in their circumstances and accepted their fate. Maybe they were weary or feeling powerless to change their situation.

Maybe they needed to see the state of their community through someone else's fresh eyes. Sometimes, when conditions are really bad, people stop noticing the trouble they're in. People are resilient, and they adapt. But Nehemiah encouraged the people to look again, to truly reckon with themselves, the state of their city, of God's city, and prepare for the work that lay ahead.

Sooner or later, as we engage in the UNDIVIDED Circle, we must take stock of where we are, where we need to be, and what needs to change to move forward. As Nehemiah said, "You see the trouble we are in."

7 The Faithful Path

John's Story

John Tanner, a pastor in Huntsville, Alabama, is working with a multiracial team of pastors and leaders in his city to advance racial healing, solidarity, and justice.

Here's his story with LivingUNDIVIDED:

Our journey in Huntsville began in the wake of the murder of George Floyd in May 2020. Like so many others in the country, we were disturbed and heartbroken by the images of that event. It led to a racial reckoning in our city and for many around the country.

In response to that, the White pastor of a larger, racially diverse church in our area organized a gathering at Big Spring Park in the heart of our city called "Praying Together for Change." A group of more than thirty diverse churches were represented, and it was a powerful evening.

Five calls to action followed Praying Together for Change. And one of the five was to form intentional partnerships between predominantly White and predominantly Black churches in our area. Another pastor and I were asked to lead this effort. We agreed early on that for these partnerships to be substantive and transformational, they needed to be built on a foundation of education and to facilitate deep and meaningful conversations on matters of race rather than the traditional pulpit-swap approach or fellowship gatherings that only scratched the surface.

That's what our LivingUNDIVIDED experience has provided—well-produced and well-facilitated events that lead to rich conversations and connections.

One of our participants said it best: "The LivingUNDIVIDED cohort was uplifting to me because it provided a place for people to have this most difficult yet necessary conversation through the lens of historical truths while managing the wide range of emotions that those truths evoke in the present."

Remember Troy's decision to show up at the chapel at Princeton after the Rodney King verdict? He made a commitment to keep showing up for racial healing, solidarity, and justice. Remember Chuck's story of watching the body cam video of the shooting of Samuel DuBose with his colleagues at the church? He wrestled with his calling and the cost of crossing the bridge to action.

These were moments of reckoning. They were filled with conflicting emotions, but they were vital to propelling us forward on our living undivided journeys.

In each case, these moments of reckoning led to seasons of reckoning.

Troy had daily conversations with a Black student named Wilmot Allen who lived in the same dorm, processing, confessing, repenting, and learning. Chuck began to speak more boldly on race at the church and brought together a team, including Troy, to form UNDIVIDED.

Real reckoning demands community, for "it is not good that . . . man should be alone" (Gen. 2:18). Community is the place of challenge, conviction, healing, confession, and repentance. As James writes, "Therefore confess your sins to one another and pray for one another, so that you may be healed. The prayer of the righteous is powerful and effective" (James 5:16). We often read this verse with an eye toward healing for the person confessing, but when it comes to the journey of living undivided, we see that when done well, the healing goes both ways. True confession, ownership of sin, and repentance in the context of authentic community can be balms of healing for all.

White people must be cautious, however, in looking to Black and Brown friends to pronounce words of forgiveness and absolution for sins of racism. This puts an unfair burden on People of Color and can at times feel like the White person is simply looking to be forgiven so they can move on.

Forgiveness must not be a way to skip over real heart work. Forgiveness shouldn't be a way to avoid behaving and living differently. No, we're talking about a true reckoning that goes much deeper. This is a change of direction, a repentance that shows up in our lives and that others can notice.

So let's define what reckoning is and is not. What it includes and does not include.

To Reckon Is Not the Same as Being Conflicted

Reckoning doesn't look like being conflicted. When a person is conflicted, they're bothered. They experience some discomfort. Being conflicted rarely leads to action. Rather, it often breeds stagnancy. And while it's a start, it's simply not enough because it's not helpful.

Being conflicted is being internally troubled but externally stoic.

Being conflicted is being overwhelmed with grief but not knowing what to say or do.

Being conflicted is knowing what's right and true and just but wrestling with having the courage to act.

Being conflicted is stepping out in boldness when first seeing the video of officer Derek Chauvin choking the life out of George Floyd, even posting strong statements on social media, and then going quiet on racial justice in the coming weeks and months.

Being conflicted is lamenting that Black, Brown, and People of Color keep leaving the organization or church but never asking why—and never making any substantive changes that would address their concerns.

Being conflicted is feeling an internal prompting to speak up when comments and decisions are made that are prejudiced or discriminatory, but out of fear of being misunderstood or labeled, remaining silent.

A few days after Dr. Martin Luther King Jr.'s home was bombed by racists in Montgomery, he preached a sermon titled "It's Hard to Be a Christian." King charged, "We have substituted a cushion for a cross. We have substituted the soothing lemonade of escape for the bitter cup of reality. We have a high blood pressure of creeds and an anemia of deeds."[1]

Let's move beyond a state of being conflicted, which is a place not of true reckoning but of deep stagnation.

To Reckon Is Not the Same as Condemnation

When we reject the temptation of being conflicted, we still have another major choice that will either take us back to stagnation or connect us with a flow of God's Spirit for racial healing and justice. The choice is between condemnation and conviction.

In Scripture, condemnation is a pronouncement of guilt (it's justice with no mercy).

Condemnation says there's no hope for us; conviction says God will help us.

Condemnation shows us only the problem; conviction shows us the answer.

Condemnation says we'll never change; conviction helps us change.

Loving mercy means we lean into the apostle Paul's words: "Therefore there is now no condemnation for those who are in Christ Jesus" (Rom. 8:1). And this conviction should lead to real-life change. When this happens, conviction moves to reckoning.

But when we do begin to truly change, we must be cautious not to fall into the trap of condemning everyone else. During the season in seminary when God was helping me (Troy) better understand my own racism and the role race plays in society, I did something many of us do when we're growing in an area: I became zealous about it. And I soon began to judge those who were not yet where I was. I became arrogant.

In this season, a friend, perhaps seeing my growing self-righteousness, encouraged me to read *Brother to a Dragonfly* by Will Campbell. Campbell was the first White board member of the Southern Christian Leadership Conference, which was led by Dr. King. He was passionate about the work for civil rights and for justice.

In the early 1960s, Campbell was a guest speaker at a gathering for the Student Nonviolent Coordinating Committee (SNCC). During the evening, the organization watched a filmstrip of a KKK training that showed poor White men, dressed in Klan garb, messing up basic instructions and turning the wrong direction. The students at the SNCC gathering laughed at the ignorance of these hate-filled Klan members. Campbell got up to speak and, before delivering his prepared remarks, challenged those who'd laughed. He told his audience that when they see people so misguided, it should break their hearts, not be cause for laughter.

Following the Rodney King verdict in the spring of 1992, I got involved in Seminarians for Justice at Princeton Seminary. The next fall, in preaching class, I decided to preach on the parable of the Pharisee and the tax collector going to the temple to pray.

In the parable, Jesus spoke to a group of people "who trusted in themselves that they were righteous and regarded others with contempt" (Luke 18:9). This description hit a little too close to home for me at the time. Jesus then told a parable that has proven to be an important reminder to us as we engage in our efforts to reckon our own personal racism.

Jesus described two men entering the temple to pray—a Pharisee (religious leader) and a tax collector (social pariah). The Pharisee prayed, "God, I thank you that I am not like other people: thieves, rogues, adulterers, or even like this tax collector. I fast twice a week; I give a tenth of all my income" (vv. 11–12).

In other words, "God, I'm awesome. We both know it."

Then we read about the tax collector's prayer. The Bible says the tax collector didn't feel worthy enough to look toward heaven. He beat his own chest as he prayed, "God, be merciful to me, a sinner!" (v. 13).

Like with any story, it's important to understand the context of Luke's account. At the time, the people of Israel viewed tax collectors as enemies of the people. Imagine an auditor for the IRS, but corrupt. They were exploiters who made handsome profits off the poor and vulnerable, aiding the Roman Empire in systemic oppression. They were the opposite of Robin Hood—they took from the poor to give to the rich. They took advantage of the desperate. Many in Israel viewed them as traitors. Even though the tax collectors themselves were Jewish, their occupation necessitated siding with Rome over the Jewish people. In fact, the Pharisees often criticized Jesus for hanging out with tax collectors and sinners.

Meanwhile, the Pharisees were the keepers of the Law and the great traditions of the Jewish faith during a time of Roman occupation. They guarded and preserved the customs and identity of the people when they were under great duress. When Jesus introduced these two characters in his story, the expectation was that the Pharisee's path was the "right" path.

In his prayer, the Pharisee focused first on other people and their shortcomings. This was a comparison game. The tax collector started with God, and then in response to God, took an honest look at himself, asking for mercy. And surprisingly, Jesus said the tax collector went home justified, because he started with a sober examination of himself.

You see, if we love mercy, how does that love extend to both people from different races or ethnicities and that crazy uncle at the family Thanksgiving?

As we reckon, let's not give in to the lie of being conflicted or the spirit of condemnation. Rather, let's lean into the gift of conviction. Reject the passivity of being conflicted. Reject condemnation. But receive the Holy Spirit's conviction. And embrace a repentance that leads to "salvation without regret" (2 Cor. 7:10 ESV).

How Did We Get Here?

In 2016, when the first LivingUNDIVIDED experience took place at Crossroads, we had twelve hundred people participate. Think about it. Twelve hundred people from one church engaging in an honest conversation about race and faith. It was incredible! To prepare for that first experience, the church did a presurvey of that group to understand where everyone was starting from. One of the questions we asked was pretty straightforward: "Have you ever had a person of a different race come to your home for dinner?"

In a large church, growing in diversity, in a city like Cincinnati, you might think the majority of the group had at one time or another had a person of a different race at their home for a meal. Especially among the first twelve hundred people to volunteer for a multiracial experience like LivingUNDIVIDED. These were the early adopters, after all! We were shocked to discover that among the twelve hundred people, nearly 50 percent had never had a person of a different race at their dinner table.

Even in a church where we gather across races, go on mission trips together, pray together, serve the community together, nearly 50 percent had never done the simple yet intimate act of sharing a meal in their home with someone racially different from them. One reason for this is that Cincinnati, like so many other cities in America, tends to be de facto segregated by race. The Urban League of Cincinnati subtitled their 2015 State of Black Cincinnati report "Two Cities," referencing the ongoing structural division of life in our city along color lines.[2]

How did we get here?

First, we have been spiritually deceived.

If we want to go back—way, way back—to the first bad decision that was made, we have to look at Adam and Eve. Genesis 3:1–6 tells the story. Satan, in the form of a serpent, sidled up to Eve and asked, "Did God say, 'You shall not eat from any tree in the garden'?" (v. 1). Eve, perhaps accustomed to chats with animals, confirmed that God had given her and Adam permission to eat from literally *any* other tree except for the one in the middle of the garden. The serpent planted one of the most insidious seeds known to man: doubt.

But the serpent said to the woman [Eve], "You will not die, for God knows that when you eat of it your eyes will be opened, and you will be like God, knowing good and evil." (vv. 4–5)

It all comes down to the serpent's question: *Did God really say . . . ?* It took only about ten seconds for the enemy to convince Eve that God wasn't being honest with her—that God was lying. Was it an actual sin to bite into the fruit? No. The sin was distrusting God and then disobeying him.

When it comes to racism and racial justice, we can fill in the blank of the serpent's question with a number of things.

Did God really say *all human beings are created in God's image?*

Did God really say *to love your neighbor as yourself?*

Did God really say *we are all one in Christ?*

Did God really say to *let justice flow down like waters and righteousness as a mighty stream?*

Satan, our spiritual enemy, is the author of division. His mission from the moment he deceived Adam and Eve was to separate humanity from communion with God and with each other. Jesus called him the "father of lies" (John 8:44), and when it comes to dividing us by race at every point of the history of the American church, too many Christians have believed the enemy's lies.

Because here's the deception we fall into: we believe God is a liar. Stay with us, here, because you'll see how this applies to racism momentarily.

It all comes down to the serpent's question: *Did God really say . . . ?*

Did God really say *all human beings are created in God's image?*

Did God really say *to love your neighbor as yourself?*

Did God really say *we are all one in Christ*?

Did God really say *to let justice flow down like waters and righteousness as a mighty stream*?

Yes, God did.

Jesus said the words *follow me* thirteen times in the Gospels. He used these two simple words to call Peter, Andrew, James, and John as his disciples. Matthew 4:18–22 tells us Jesus was out walking beside the Sea of Galilee when he saw Peter and Andrew fishing. Jesus said, "Follow me, and I will make you fishers of people" (v. 19). Peter and Andrew immediately followed.

Then Jesus encountered James and John. He called to them and they, too, followed. The same was true for Matthew.

> As Jesus was walking along, he saw a man called Matthew sitting at the tax-collection station, and he said to him, "Follow me." And he got up and followed him. (9:9)

Jesus invited these men to become not only his disciples but also his friends and the cornerstone of his future church. He didn't ask them to prove their righteousness or how well they'd kept the Law. He didn't even ask them what they thought of him being the Messiah. All he said was, "Follow me."

We want to ask you to do the same thing. No, not follow us. Follow Jesus—follow his words. Follow his stories. Follow his character. If there's something you've read about the American church's history of racism that surprised you, wounded you, or made you angry, good. Now's the time to reckon with what God is revealing. You have the opportunity to reject weariness and powerlessness. You're ready for a journey of racial healing, solidarity, and justice.

Let's continue this journey together.

Reclaiming What's Been Lost

Think about what it would be like if someone were to steal your identity. Maybe that's happened to you. You checked your credit card statement and saw charges from a different state or country that you didn't make. I (Troy) once found multiple charges, some as large as eighty dollars, on my debit card to a restaurant called Whataburger, a Texas-based hamburger chain. I had never eaten at Whataburger, and I knew I had never dropped that type of coin at the local White Castle. The charges had to belong to someone else. I felt violated that someone had seized my identity and used it for a burger joint. The least they could have done was bought some good Texas BBQ!

Have you had a situation like this happen to you? Or can you imagine it? Makes your blood boil, doesn't it? You would immediately call your credit card company or the authorities and make a report. You wouldn't drop it either. You'd see the complaint through until what was taken from you was restored.

What if I told you something that belongs to you *has* been taken? That part of your identity—a God-given, God-ordained piece of who you are—has been ripped away from you? In fact, it's been gone so long that you don't even know it's missing.

What are we talking about? Your identity as a member of God's multiracial church. We're talking about a right relationship with all members of God's family—a relationship God envisioned for us once the church itself was established in the book of Acts.

The apostle Paul picked up on this when he spoke to the people of Athens: "From one ancestor he made all peoples to inhabit the whole earth" (Acts 17:26). The translation of this text in the NKJV is even more poignant: "And He has made from *one blood* every nation" (emphasis added). Put simply, from the very beginning, God created humanity to live undivided—to love courageously, without bounds.

God created us to belong to one another. That's our true identity as followers of Jesus. Together, let's reclaim what's been lost.

When we reclaim this shared identity, we can also reckon with the myriad ways in which we have historically, as a nation and even as the church, attacked the God-given identities of Black, Indigenous, and other People of Color. When we reclaim what has been lost, we can also reckon with the impact it has had on our Black, Brown, Asian Pacific Islander, and Indigenous kindred.

Images Are Sticky

A few years ago, my (Chuck's) father passed away. I loved my dad dearly, and it was (and still is) a deep loss in my life. He lived to be ninety-one years old.

As I shared earlier in the book, my dad grew up in the midst of segregation, which made him a very tough person. He came to faith in Jesus later in life, a few years after I was born, and served as a deacon in the church I grew up in. But to use a term from the Black church, my dad had quite a wild "BC" life (BC meaning "before Christ"). From working on the railroads to running a speakeasy in the heart of Philadelphia to a stint (or two) in jail, my dad lived a life full of twists and turns that shaped him into the man who raised me.

Despite the challenges he faced and the decisions he wished he could take back, my dad lived to see me graduate from college, work at a *Fortune* 100 company, and pastor a large, growing church. Even more special to him, though, was getting to enjoy his role as "Pop Pop" with my three young children. My dad was very proud of me. And I will always love and admire him.

My dad served in the Army and was stationed in Europe during the Korean War. It's from this time in his life that one of my favorite pictures of him was taken. In the picture, my dad, in his midtwenties, is standing on the front of his Army-issued Jeep, looking like one cool customer! He's got a cigarette dangling from his mouth, one hand on his hip, and just looks like he's living his best life.

He also looks like a man you don't want to cross! That image captures Dad's indomitable spirit more than any other photo I have of him. It also captures his mischievous side, which was always on display in our relationship. That image literally speaks thousands of words about the man I knew, loved, and still very much miss every day.

Images have a way of being sticky. Sometimes more than words, sometimes even more than actions, images linger in our minds. We associate emotions with images. We associate seasons of life with images. Think about flipping through pictures of your kids when they were younger, or pictures from your high school or college years. Each image stirs up a memory—a moment. Images are important.

Because we're followers of Jesus, our sacred text begins in the very first chapter of Genesis with the assertion that all human beings are created by God and in God's image: "So God created humans in his image, in the image of God he created them; male and female he created them" (Gen. 1:27).

We share an image with God. All of us. When we look in the spiritual mirror, we should see the same loving Father staring back at us. In our lives, that shared image should be our beacon—our guiding light of reasoning in how we carry ourselves and treat others.

I Am Somebody

When Dr. Martin Luther King Jr. was young, like most preacher's kids, he wasn't always eager to hear his father, the Rev. Martin Luther King Sr., preach every Sunday morning at Ebenezer Baptist Church. He and a friend would occasionally sneak out of church, but not to roam the neighborhood or stir up trouble. Instead, they would make their way a few short blocks down Auburn Avenue to Wheat Street Baptist Church, where they would sit in the balcony and hear the esteemed Rev. William Holmes Borders preach. Martin Luther King Jr. was mesmerized by the way this dynamic preacher used his whole body and spun words together. His sermons touched on a broad range of topics, including segregation, patriotism (during WWII), and the northern migration of Black people in those times. In fact, some would later note that part of King's flair for oratory was very much "in the image" of Reverend Borders.

Borders's more famous refrain for his Black congregation was the bold proclamation: "I am somebody!" He later turned this into a poem,[3] and years later, a young Reverend Jesse Jackson began using a version of the poem in sermons, speeches, and even on a 1972 episode of *Sesame Street*, where he invited a group of young children on set and on television screens around the nation to cry out each phrase in response. Go ahead and google Jesse Jackson and *Sesame Street*, and see if you don't get chills:

I am somebody! I am somebody! I may be poor, but I am somebody. I may be young, but I am somebody. I may be on welfare, but I am somebody. I may be small, but I am somebody. I may have made mistakes, but I am somebody. My clothes are different, my face is different, my hair is different, but I am somebody. I am Black, Brown, or White. I speak a different language. But I must be respected, protected, never rejected. I am God's child! I am somebody.[4]

176

Borders's poem and Jackson's recitation in the early days of *Sesame Street* were both countercultural declarations rooted in the power of Genesis 1:27. They were a claiming, or reclaiming, of our roots. It's no accident that Alex Haley's epic book and miniseries on the Black experience from Africa to the United States is called *Roots*.

As the children cry out "I am somebody" and "I am God's child," they aren't doing so in isolation. If I am somebody, then my neighbor is somebody, the person of a different race is somebody, and even my enemy is somebody.

In the story of Adam and Eve, God's decision to create Eve is in response to something amiss: "It is not good that the man should be alone" (Gen. 2:18). Humans are made for community across differences. One could rightly say it's in our bones: "And the rib that the LORD God had taken from the man he made into a woman and brought her to the man. Then the man said, 'This at last is bone of my bones and flesh of my flesh'" (vv. 22–23).

When we're truly aligned with God's design, the idea of belonging to one another should indeed be in our bones.

The Truth That Sets Us Free

I (Troy) love to cook—the kitchen is one place where I can rejuvenate and unplug from challenges, worries, and tasks left undone. I immerse myself in the recipe and the process. When I get a meal right, as an achiever on the Enneagram (#3), I have an immense feeling of accomplishment and pride. And then there are the many times when I come up short. The cooking takes longer than expected, particularly on my smoker, and dinner isn't on the table until nearly 8:00 p.m., when we were hoping to eat at 6:30 p.m.

A few years ago on Christmas Eve, we were planning a big meal with our children and my parents for that evening. For lunch we decided to do a light meal featuring a homemade tomato soup in our Vitamix blender. It's pretty cool—the force of the blender actually heats and cooks the soup. And then I began sharing the soup with my family. My mother said it was amazing, but my children, who pull no punches, said, "Dad, this tastes like watered-down Campbell's tomato soup!"

Then I realized I had left out the ingredient that would have brought the flavor we were missing—a jar of garlic-seasoned sun-dried tomatoes. It was there on the counter, right where I could not miss it, and yet I did.

The Western church, and particularly the church in the United States, has often viewed racial solidarity, healing, and justice as optional ingredients. You can add them to the sauce if you choose, but they aren't essential, and in fact, they can be distractions from the true gospel or the good news of Jesus. This assertion is grounded in a notion that God is ultimately concerned about the individual's personal relationship with God.

This is true but incomplete. God's best for his people is so much more than a personal transaction with him, a version of Monopoly's "Get Out of Jail Free" card reimagined as a "Get Out of Hell Free" card. Jesus is inviting us into so much more.

As followers of Jesus, we can be a racially reconciled community of grace and truth. We have an opportunity to embody the mission of Jesus in this way. We have a *calling* to embody the mission of Jesus in this way. It is not a job to be done but a gift to be received and enjoyed.

Even though we have often failed, God has uniquely empowered the church to lead on race. Far too many have abused and persecuted others based on race in Jesus's name. But there has always been a remnant who has built bridges, pursued reconciliation, and worked for justice, and this righteous remnant is grounded in the DNA of the church and what it means to truly follow Jesus.

Brian and Mario

Brian Dershaw and Mario Stuckey are two men who completed the LivingUNDIVIDED experience and went on to be cofacilitators for other groups engaged in the program. Mario is Black, and Brian is White.

When people are paired to facilitate, they typically don't know each other prior to being assigned. Mario and Brian decided to not only serve together but also *respond* to each other. They met for coffee before leading their first session, and what blossomed out of that one step toward each other has transformed their lives and had a ripple effect on countless others.

Mario says, "What surprised me most about Brian was the irony of all the things we had in common. We share the same birthday, our kids are around the same ages, we're both from families of six, and we even had the same first job."

See? There really are more similarities than differences among God's children. And not just in quirky commonalities, but in the desire to connect to one another in a meaningful way.

Mario and Brian didn't stop showing up for each other. Over the next few years, they continued to meet. To talk. To share. They were vulnerable. And now they consider each other family. Why? Because Mario took the courageous step of taking off the veil. Because Brian demonstrated not only curiosity but also a deep concern for Mario. Because they learned that they are better together, serving across differences, than they are apart. Because they took the chance to be wrong, the chance to be offended, and the chance to care about someone who looked different from them.

By the way, it's worth mentioning that most of this relationship-building took place over the course of 2020, when White and Black men seemingly had every reason to create space between themselves. Brian and Mario dug in deeper and leaned into and on each other, creating a safe space for both men to process their grief, fear, and pain.

Notice that Brian and Mario didn't engage with each other from a position of power. No, their approach was to build a true, reciprocal friendship.

We also saw the power of reckoning in a group of Jesus followers praying on courthouse steps in the middle of social unrest, producing peace and nonviolence explainable only by the power of Jesus. We've seen it in a maximum-security prison where a former Black Panther enforcer and a former skinhead went through our experience and formed a deep brotherhood. We've seen it through the historic passage of a school levy that enabled thousands of poor Black and Brown children to gain access to quality preschool.

We've all been invited, as members of God's family, into this ministry of reconciliation. We don't *have* to do this. We *get* to do this!

We believe the time is now for another movement of people of faith toward racial solidarity and justice. And as we will discuss in the next chapter, we have all the power we need to bring about the change we want to see.

Respond and Reckon

Jesus is our best example of someone who loves mercy. Fresh off a trip to the Mount of Olives, Jesus went to the temple early one morning. Soon a crowd had gathered around to hear him teach. As he was speaking, the teachers of the religious law (the Pharisees) brought up a woman who had been caught in the act of adultery. They placed her center stage—right in front of the crowd. "Teacher, this woman was caught in the very act of committing adultery. Now in the law Moses commanded us to stone such women. Now what do you say?" (John 8:4–5).

There's nothing formulaic about Jesus's response. We know from John's account that the stage gradually emptied until the only two left were Jesus and the woman. He didn't condemn her, but he said, "Go your way, and from now on do not sin again" (v. 11). His merciful response contained both a rejection of sin and a mandate to live righteously. Mercy isn't dishonest. But mercy does speak in love.

The Pharisees who dragged the woman before Jesus had intended to set a trap to use his words against him (John 8:5–6). The wisdom in Jesus's words to the woman both circumvented their plan and exemplified the position of mercy according to Jesus. This wasn't the first instance when Jesus chose mercy in front of the Pharisees. In several recorded encounters between them, Jesus cited Hosea 6:6: "I desire mercy, not sacrifice" (Matt. 9:13; see also 12:7).

In John's narrative of the judgmental mob, Jesus demonstrated what is good. The religious leaders asked that the woman be stoned according to Moses's law. But Jesus didn't allow that. Jesus was a stone catcher. That's the kind of mercy we're called to—the stone-catching kind.

The mercy we are to love is also translated as "faithfulness" or "lovingkindness." The word *mercy* occurs nearly 250 times in Scripture, mostly when describing a quality of how God deals with people. Yet a quarter of its usage refers to the merciful qualities there are, or there should be, between God's people. It stands to reason that God's lovingkindness toward us gives us a basis for our mercy toward others. A mercy that invites us to respond to one another across differences and leads us to reckon with a new and better way forward—as one humanity.

EXAMINE YOUR STORY

Read 2 Corinthians 7:10.

1. When have you experienced godly sorrow over racism?
2. How do you move from conflicted to convicted?
3. How has your soul been wounded through racism?
   What next step can you take to pursue a path of
   healing?

PART 5

RESTORE

DO JUSTICE

5. RESTORE—Taking action to repair wounds and cultivate systems in which all people flourish.

6. RESOLVE

Justice is one of those words whose connotation is deeply connected to personal experience. That's why the idea of "doing" justice may be the most daunting of all the actions listed in Micah's reminder of what God says is good. How can we "do" the very thing we've been longing for and thirsting for ourselves?

Let's take a step back and revisit the Scripture itself:

> He has told you, O mortal, what is good,
> and what does the LORD require of you
> but to do justice and to love kindness
> and to walk humbly with your God? (Mic. 6:8)

Remember, the verses represent a conversation between God and Israel through the prophet Micah. In the first five verses, God makes his case against the disobedient people of Israel. Israel's focus was on the external—their religious sacrificial practices. Verses 6–7 summarize their response to God's indictment: Just *what* did God want from them that would be satisfactory enough to cover their sin?

Verse 8 follows with God's answer: he has already told them what's good. In other words, Israel already should have known the answer to their questions. God didn't want religious practices—God wanted justice, mercy, and humility.

We've already drawn a correlation between Israel and the current state of our world, but what about you personally? Is serving in church more important to you than standing up for the marginalized? Is tithing a more pressing priority than sharing in the grief of a friend of Color? Does leading a small group take precedence over speaking out against racial injustice?

The very first item on the list of doing good, the very first action God requires, is to *do justice*. Micah's audience would've understood this to mean acting for others out of a sense of right and wrong. In particular, the judicial courts had a responsibility to provide equal treatment and protect the innocent—they had a responsibility to provide procedural justice. How were they doing?

> Woe to those who devise wickedness
>   and evil deeds on their beds!
> When the morning dawns, they perform it,
>   because it is in their power.
> They covet fields and seize them;
>   houses and take them away;
> they oppress householder and house,
>   people and their inheritance. (Mic. 2:1–2)

It's a safe inference that injustice was a problem in Israel at that time. Thousands of years later, have we really come very far? Let's do something different. Let's do justice.

Justice is the mantle Nehemiah chose to take up in defense of the marginalized Jewish community in Jerusalem. When some of the surrounding rulers heard that the Jewish people were repairing the city walls and gates, they did what a lot of bullies do—they started to make fun of the Jews' efforts, likely because they were afraid of what might happen if the momentarily weaker party succeeded. One of those rulers, Sanballat, said,

> What are these feeble Jews doing? Will they restore it by themselves? Will they offer sacrifice? Will they finish it in a day? Will they revive the stones out of the heaps of rubbish—burned ones at that? (Neh. 4:2)

Instead of being deterred by their taunts and sneers, Nehemiah and his crew bore down harder:

> So we rebuilt the wall, and all the wall was joined together to half its height, for the people had a mind to work. (v. 6)

"The people had a mind to work." That's exactly what it takes to do justice—a mind to do the hard work of restoration. It also takes an activation of power. Remember, earlier in Nehemiah, he'd called on God for strength: "Give success to your servant today, and grant him mercy in the sight of this man!" (1:11).

Nehemiah explicitly connected the power of God to the very real power dynamics of his situation and context. That was the moment Nehemiah started building power. And it was through that same power that the people constructed the wall that was vital to the protection and flourishing of Jerusalem, restoring the city to safety and honor.

Step Five: Restore

Our vision is a flow of racial healing and justice that repairs wounds and cultivates equitable systems where all people flourish.

In the words of Sanballat, "Will they restore things?"

We think so.

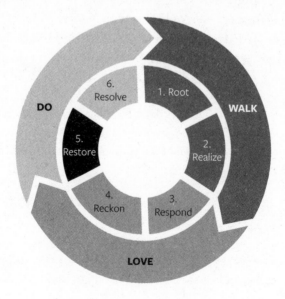

8 Power Supply

After Nehemiah became rooted in his identity as a child of God, he realized he had a role to play in the problem *and* solution to the crisis his brothers and sisters in Jerusalem were enduring. He responded to the king he served, sharing his heart for his people openly and vulnerably. Nehemiah reckoned with the destruction in his city, gathering its people and creating a plan of action for repairing the systemic and structural destruction that surrounded them.

Sounds great, right? Sounds inspiring.

Wouldn't it be nice if we saw problems like systemic racism and immediately had access to the resources to bring resolution?

One thing Nehemiah had that we don't is access to one of the richest rulers in the world's treasure chest. If you feel inadequate linking arms with your neighbor to love mercy—to relate and reckon—let us assure you that you have something far more valuable than a fistful of letters of passage and carts filled with lumber.

You have what it takes to rebuild.

In early spring 2019, I (Chuck) was downstairs in my house starting a quiet morning with some reading, when all of a sudden, I heard a loud *pop!* It sounded like a bomb had gone off, and within a few minutes, my wife and three kids were up and we were all wondering what the heck had just happened. Turns out, a transformer exploded in the back of our house. Within a few hours, and still in darkness, the Duke Energy trucks started showing up on our street to fix the problem.

While that part was normal, what wasn't normal was having so many members of the crew huddling in our backyard with puzzled looks on their faces. I threw on my slippers and ran outside to see what was up. They told me the transformer was connected to an underground power line and that line had been damaged by the explosion. Then they told me the power line ran right through my backyard.

This meant that over the next week they'd have to bring in backhoes and other heavy equipment to dig up our backyard and repair the power line. Now, while it was definitely a bit of an inconvenience, it also provided the best entertainment you could imagine for young kids. Every morning, the crew would bring these huge vehicles up our driveway and dig a hole in our backyard while my kids watched from the comfort of our raised back patio.

The hole eventually got to be about seven or eight feet deep, and then the real fun began. They took apart the old pipe, piece by piece, and then brought in the new pipe to replace it. I have to admit that my kids weren't the only ones who were mesmerized at our very own real-life episode of *Bob the Builder*. Eventually, the repair was finished and the power was restored. But that experience gave me an even greater appreciation of the importance (and intricacy) of our power grid.

The same can be said for our potential for power to address the spiritual sin of racism and its personal, relational, institutional, and systemic effects in our society. We hold so much potential for powerful changes—but we must realize the potential of our power grid if we want to see racial healing, solidarity, and justice flow in our churches, communities, and world.

Because we are followers of Jesus, wired and equipped to be radical world-changers, that's exactly the position many of us today find ourselves in. We've been given the most transformative power in all of creation—the unending, unchanging, unfathomable love of Christ. That's our greatest superpower. But will we use it, or will we continue to be stagnant and impotent against injustice?

Romans 8:38–39 says, "For I am convinced that neither death, nor life, nor angels, nor rulers, nor things present, nor things to come, nor powers, nor height, nor depth, nor anything else in all creation will be able to separate us from the love of God in Christ Jesus our Lord."

The power of God's love is immeasurable. It's bigger than life *and* death. Bigger than anything in the past *or* the future. There's no depth that can affect God's love. No height. The power of God's love is the single most compelling force known (or unknown) to man. Guess what? That incredible, amazing, life-changing, soul-altering love lives inside of *you*. You have full access to it. You can unplug from the power source of your own logic, experience, and emotions, and you can upgrade your power grid by tapping into God's.

The Most Durable Power

In 1956, while Martin Luther King Jr. was the pastor of Dexter Avenue Baptist Church in Montgomery, he delivered a sermon titled "The Most Durable Power." Now, remember that by that time, King and the Black community of Montgomery had been boycotting city buses for eleven months! The Supreme Court hadn't yet given their monumental ruling saying segregated buses were unconstitutional. It would've been easy for King, his congregation, and the broader Black community to give up. But King urged them on with the following words:

I still believe that love is the most durable power in the world.[1]

Remember, we are defining love as ascribing worth to others, even at cost to yourself. Over and over again in the Bible we read about the power of love (cue the Huey Lewis and the News song). For example, 1 Corinthians 13:13, where Paul says, "And now these three remain: faith, hope and love. But the greatest of these is love" (NIV). Paul is writing here about the most durable things God has graced the church to possess: faith, hope, and love. *But the greatest of these is love.*

Fear of the Other

Why do we believe racial healing, solidarity, and justice are possible? Why is it not a mere pipe dream? Because followers of Jesus have been imbued with the most durable power in the universe, and that power enables them to achieve these purposes.

One more verse to consider is 1 John 4:18, which says this: "There is no fear in love, but perfect love casts out fear; for fear has to do with punishment, and whoever fears has not reached perfection in love." One of the underlying reasons racism and injustice have been perpetuated over the years is fear-based narratives of the "other." When you can make someone believe a certain group of people poses an existential threat to your "life, liberty, and happiness" or that of your children, it's not long before you can justify anything, including race-based violence and oppression, to protect yourself or those you love from them. This story has played out all over the world.

However, the way of love offers a powerful alternative to fear, hatred, and violence. But power isn't a "name it and claim it" kind of resource. Let's break down what power is, because we often get it twisted. We associate power with corruption, oppression, something distasteful. But power actually means the ability to act. Dr. King puts a finer point on power, defining it as "the ability to achieve purpose."[2]

If you think about it, much of what leads to oppression, injustice, and evil in the world is the imposition of powerlessness on a group of people. Racism is rooted in disempowering people by restricting their movement, narrowing their opportunities, and minimizing their voices. To make matters worse, often someone figures out a way to profit off the conditions of Black, Brown, and Indigenous people. This is true of slavery, Jim Crow segregation, removing access to voting rights, and limiting access to education. All these impose powerlessness on people.

Road Map to Power

One aspect of our racial history as a country that's worth revisiting, celebrating, and applying to our present moment is that the Black community and other communities of Color, even when under duress due to racism, have never been fully powerless. And their examples provide a critical road map for how we can effectively build and wield power for healing and justice in the world today.

Lean on God

Long before Europeans forcibly kidnapped and brought Africans to the shores of America, many were Christians and part of the church that Jesus established. It's quite possible that some of the enslaved Africans brought to America were already followers of Jesus. While the slave owners hoped to equate Christianity with Paul's admonition, "Slaves, obey your earthly masters" (Eph. 6:5), God cannot be limited to one verse. The enslaved learned other stories. They learned Jesus conquered death. They learned God delivered God's people from bondage in Egypt. They learned the walls of Jericho came tumbling down. They learned God is a God of deliverance, freedom, justice, and power.

They created new worship songs, which today we call spirituals, celebrating these very aspects of God's nature. And they would regularly "steal away" to a distant part of the plantation to worship, sing, dance, and proclaim the power of God through Jesus. By leaning on God and his track record of deliverance, they knew God hated the oppression they were under, and that with him, they had hope that a new day could come.

This hope in God undergirded the Civil Rights Movement. In one of the most pivotal moments of the 1960s, just a few weeks after Alabama State Troopers pummeled John Lewis and dozens of others on the Edmund Pettus Bridge in Selma, King joined Lewis and hundreds of leaders throughout the nation in a march from Selma to Montgomery. When they finally arrived at their destination, after several days of heavy rains along the way, King addressed the crowd with a message rooted in the power of God. He recited the chorus of an old Negro spiritual, "Joshua Fit the Battle of Jericho":

> Joshua fit the battle of Jericho,
> Joshua fit the battle of Jericho,
> And the walls come tumbling down.
> Up to the walls of Jericho they marched, spear in hand.
> "Go blow them ram horns," Joshua cried,
> "'Cause the battle am in my hand."

Then King said, "These words I have given you just as they were given us by the unknown, long-dead, dark-skinned originator. Some now long-gone black bard bequeathed to posterity these words in ungrammatical form, yet with emphatic pertinence for all of us today."[3]

King was inviting the people to lean on God, the God who won the battle of Jericho and inspired a "long-dead, dark-skinned originator" to have hope that God could bring deliverance yet again. As activists made a final push for voting rights, King delivered a speech titled "Our God Is Marching On."[4] Less than five months later, President Johnson signed the Voting Rights Act.[5]

In the struggle for racial healing and justice, we find power, or the ability to achieve purpose, by remembering the God who delivers and has delivered—both in Scripture and throughout human history. This is where we find hope to contest for justice in the world.

Build Power in Love

Remember, power is the ability to act or achieve purpose. While leaning on God is vital to believing change is possible, one also has to be willing to take action.

These dynamics are true in Black history as well. When Richard Allen decided to reject the racism and White supremacy of his White-led congregation, he started building power. He organized the Black community to launch their own congregation: Bethel African Methodist Episcopal Church in Philadelphia. He raised resources to sustain the new congregation and fund their first building.

But Richard Allen didn't stop there. With God's help, he kept building, launching the first Black-led denomination in the United States—the African Methodist Episcopal Church.

Along with Absalom Jones, he established a mutual aid society, called the Free African Society, to support the Black community. Allen built power.

The Civil Rights Movement was rooted in organizing people and resources, from enlisting fifty thousand people in Montgomery to stay off the buses for a full year to organizing a vast movement of college students to sit in at segregated businesses. Children in Birmingham faced dogs and fire hoses and filled up the jails, and as many as twenty-five thousand brave souls boldly crossed the Edmund Pettus Bridge. People put their bodies on the line for justice. Without these courageous acts, rooted in building power, the Civil Rights Movement would not have happened.

As followers of Jesus, we're often very comfortable talking about the power of God, but our inability to build power through organizing people and resources is one of the largest impediments to change.

Let us be crystal clear: social media posts, podcasts, sermons, book studies, T-shirts, and yard signs may affect the environment and narrative, and they are important, but alone they will accomplish nothing if there isn't a concrete strategy to build collective power to address injustice.

As we prepare to focus on doing justice, we will dive deeper into the practical ways we can build the power we need in these perilous days. The power to move out of stagnancy and join God's flow of racial healing and justice.

9   What Does the Lord Require of You?

The preamble to Micah's list in Micah 6:8 is the beginning of a question: "And what does the Lord require of you?" Those words often get lost when unpacking Micah 6:8. But they're important.

If I were to ask you to make a list right now of what God requires of his followers, what would you say? Would reading the Bible be on it? Tithing? Weekly church attendance? Volunteering might make your list. I bet if I'd asked you to make a list of what God requires of you prior to reading Micah 6:8, you wouldn't have rushed to add "do justice." Why? Because it's a high calling. It's one our country can't seem to get right. And it hasn't been a priority in many churches. So how can we get it right?

The Choice to Do

We recognize that even if you agree with 100 percent of what you've read so far, that doesn't necessarily translate into real change in the lives of others unless you have the courage to act—to *do* something.

Our country and the church are in a season of deep polarization. Our fears have convinced us that we understand one another less and less and that we have less and less in common. But no matter where we are in the racial mosaic of our country, we can do something.

The AMOS Project

Over a decade ago, when I (Troy) was still pastoring at University Christian Church, I got involved in the AMOS Project, a collection of congregations committed to racial and economic justice in the metro area of Cincinnati. In 2010, we learned that Cincinnati had an unwritten rule that people with felony convictions couldn't get civil service jobs—or in other words, good-paying jobs—working for the city.

We learned about the problem through the story of Gene Mays. As a teen, Mays was a great athlete and had scholarship offers to play college basketball. But he made a bad decision and was caught smoking weed in the school parking lot. He was suspended from school and thrown off the basketball team, and he lost his scholarship offers. He then descended into years of addiction and spent time in prison.

Several years later, Gene had a moment of clarity. He wanted to be a good father and husband and knew it was time for a change. God intervened, and he left his life of drug addiction behind. He joined an apprenticeship program to become an electrician and earned the highest marks of any student in his class year after year. When he finally finished his apprenticeship, he applied for a job with the city of Cincinnati. But just before he began work, the city discovered he had a felony on his record. He lost the job before he'd even started. Gene learned the hard way that despite having paid his debt to society, second chances didn't apply to jobs with the city of Cincinnati.

We heard Gene's story, and through AMOS, churches around the city partnered with the Ohio Justice and Policy Center to push the city council to adopt a fair-hiring policy. If passed, the measure would ban the felony box from city job applications, meaning the city could not ask up front whether a person had been convicted of a felony.

This campaign to change the hiring practices of the City of Cincinnati offered me a hands-on lesson about the difference between mobilizing and organizing. In the late 1980s, historian Charles Payne penned an essay on Civil Rights icon Ella Baker that elevates the distinction. Baker had worked as field organizer for the South for the NAACP in the 1940s, led the day-to-day of the Southern Christian Leadership Conference with Martin Luther King Jr. in the late 1950s, and shepherded the Student Nonviolent Coordinating Committee and leaders like John Lewis in the 1960s. Payne writes, "Organizing, according to Ella Baker, involves creating ongoing groups that are mass-based in the sense that the people the group purports to represent have real impact on the group's direction. Mobilizing is more sporadic, involving large numbers of people for relatively short periods of time and probably for relatively dramatic activities."[1]

The Montgomery Bus Boycott was organizing, with the people together engaged in a long struggle for justice that included accountability to the very people who refused to ride the buses. The March on Washington was mobilizing. The March from Selma to Montgomery, following Bloody Sunday in 1965, was mobilizing layered on top of organizing in Selma over the years, as people came across the country for dramatic action. Most protests and marches, particularly after another tragic video chronicling the senseless death of a Black person, are mobilizing. Both are important. Mobilizing can change the narrative and atmosphere. Organizing can, over time, channel power to make sustainable change.

Our work with AMOS was organizing work, with long campaigns rooted in clear constituencies. In 2010, the core constituency included formerly incarcerated people who had felony convictions on their record, coupled with faith leaders and congregations in Cincinnati.

Early in 2010, the majority of the city council and the mayor were unwilling to move on this effort. They pointed out that the nation was still in the throes of the Great Recession, and nobody would support giving jobs to "felons" and "ex-cons." Well, as followers of Jesus, we believed deeply in redemption and second chances and started pushing our city to do the same.

After a public meeting of several hundred people, we planned to go en masse to the Civil Service Commission meeting at city hall the next day, which was scheduled to include public comment. They learned we were coming and decided at the last minute to suspend public comment.

We showed up anyway and sat through the public part of the meeting, minus the opportunity for us to speak. Then the Civil Service Commission announced they were going into private session, and the seventy-five of us who'd gathered to raise our voices were told we had to leave the premises. A sheriff's deputy even moved to the front of the room and instructed us to leave immediately.

At that moment, I knew I had a choice to make. As I looked around and saw new friends who happened to be returning citizens being dismissed and silenced and rejected yet again, I knew I couldn't be silent. I stood up, trembling and quaking, and walked to the front of the room, ignoring the sheriff's instructions, and the people followed. I didn't look at the officer but instead looked at the three commissioners and let them know we demanded to be heard. And I asked for only two minutes. Just two minutes for them to hear from their constituency. And the commissioners relented.

I took the first minute and simply recounted famous "felons" from the Bible, like Moses, Daniel, Joseph, Paul, Peter, and even Jesus himself. I suggested that I hoped our city would have a job for Jesus if he showed up, and that according to Matthew 25, maybe when we reject jobs for those on the margins, we are rejecting Jesus. I then turned over what remained of our time to an attorney who shared how other cities were moving ahead with fair-hiring policies and how Cincinnati could easily join them.

By August, the city council unanimously passed the first city fair-hiring policy in Ohio. Over the coming few years, cities across the state joined in, and finally the state passed its own statewide ordinance, but it started with a group of congregations and returning citizens collectively deciding to do justice.

Doing justice requires acting in the public arena and inevitably demands overcoming our fears, uncertainties, and feelings of inadequacy. If you want to connect to God's flow for racial healing, tap into the power of God and *do* justice.

Seeking Justice

Nehemiah's example, and our experiences with UNDIVIDED, show us that doing justice can take place on multiple levels.

Intrapersonal (How Race Affects Us Internally)

Nehemiah was thoughtful in his own leadership and practices to ensure that he was not acting unjustly toward the vulnerable and marginalized. When we do justice at this level, we commit to this same thoughtfulness and consistency of action. For some, this means building cultural competency so we understand the issues of racial division and injustice and can work to counteract them in our spheres of influence. This is also where we come to understand that justice is an expression of our Christian faith and not an optional aspect of what it means to follow Jesus faithfully. We commit to embodying justice as part of our apprenticeship to Jesus.

For some of us, justice at this level is more about our own personal healing journey. Racism hurts us all, particularly those who have been victimized or marginalized by either direct offenses or oppressive systems. Our LivingUNDIVIDED experiences, under the leadership of Courtney Walton, have begun to elevate the need and opportunity for intrapersonal reflection and healing. We're learning that for justice to roll down like waters, there must be space for healing to flow into our own wounded hearts. Doing justice includes pursuing healing, practicing seasons of healthy pause, and finding joy and meaning through safe spaces and trusted relationships that help us show up more whole in our lives.

Interpersonal (How Race Affects Us Relationally)

Nehemiah was in community as he did justice in Israel. He was in community with both those who were similar to him in terms of their influence and those who were different. He wasn't stuck in his stagnant echo chamber. Similarly, as we seek to do justice at the interpersonal level, we commit to being in spaces where we're engaging in healthy racial discourse and finding common cause with not only those who look like us but also those who look different. As we commit to crossing racial relationships with purpose and accountability, we're better able to act justly and effect change.

Institutional (How Race Affects Organizations)

Nehemiah was an institutional leader. He was preparing the culture for restoration, and many of his reforms were at the institutional level because institutions have the power to shape culture for individuals. Some of you are institutional leaders. You may be a pastor, a business owner, a public official, the principal of a school, or the leader of a nonprofit organization. Sadly, many institutions in our country still place the preferences and norms of White culture at the center of how they operate, even as their constituents are increasingly diverse.

Perhaps you find it difficult to recruit and retain diverse talent because of cultural obstacles that Black, Indigenous, and People of Color face in your organization (or perhaps in your industry as a whole). Institutional leaders do justice by practicing the courage, curiosity, and patience needed to confront the legacy and prevalence of White supremacy and anti-Blackness in their institutions and replace them with a culture that truly embodies living undivided and with equitable systems where all people flourish.

Effecting Systemic Change

One of the great things about my (Troy's) upbringing is the centrality and importance of the Bible. In sixth grade, my Sunday school teacher established a contest, and whoever got the most points received a free ticket to Kings Island, which is the amusement park of record in my part of the Midwest. And so I was committed. If we showed up for Sunday school, we got a point. And if we read the Bible every day for that week, we got a point.

I started reading the Bible every day. It should come as a surprise to no one who understands my thirst for knowledge to hear that I won the contest. The night before the trip to Kings Island, I was so amped up that I didn't sleep. I got up the next morning sick and vomiting and ended up not being able to go.

I did get a lousy T-shirt that said The Beast on it, which is the name of the iconic roller coaster at the park.

But one thing that came out of that Sunday school contest was an intentionality about reading the Bible. It's a discipline that has stuck with me since the age of twelve.

A few years later in youth group, we watched a video series by Dr. Tony Campolo of Eastern University called "You Can Make a Difference." Tony talked about poverty, justice, race—things I had never heard one word about in my church. And as he talked about these things, I thought, *Wait a second. Dr. Campolo is right. That's all over the Bible I've been reading every day for the last five years.* Yes. God is a God who desires a personal relationship with us through Jesus. And God is a God of justice, and the Bible is filled with that call.

Take the Next Step

If God is indeed a God of justice, what is the pathway to truly join in his work of justice in our communities today? Let's go back to the importance of building power rooted in love. If building power through organized people and resources is necessary for doing justice in the world, we must take the following four vital steps:

1. *Decide.* Nothing can replace the bold decision to act in the world. This step takes courage. It takes commitment. And it makes all the difference. Oh, by the way, this isn't a one-time deal. Deciding to do justice is a daily decision. Dr. King received death threats almost every day for the last dozen years of his life. He had to decide each and every morning that he would struggle for justice.

2. *Connect*. We must get in relationship with others if we're going to build the power necessary to change racist systems and structures. There are no shortcuts. In our work for justice, we know that it's vital to build trusting and meaningful relationships.

Practically speaking, this means several cups of coffee (or tea), breakfasts, lunches, or Zoom calls shared every month. This means we're hungry to meet people and eager to get to know their passion, calling, pain, and hopes. This requires deep listening, embodying a spirit of curiosity and care, and being fully present during these meetings.

If all that comes from a meeting is being fully present with another person created in God's image for forty-five minutes on a Tuesday afternoon, let us suggest that this is an act of healing and justice. It's rare to meet someone who's truly interested in us and not trying to sell us something or recruit us.

Sometimes this is where the relationship ends. We learn our interests or concerns aren't aligned, so we bless each other and move on. This may sound callous, but think about it. Jesus met thousands of people but chose to deeply invest in only a dozen or so.

But there are also meetings when something opens up for both people, and we see a path of collective action together in the world. We may choose to meet again, or maybe we see a chance to invite the other person into a shared action.

3. *Challenge*. To build the power we need to truly do justice, we must challenge people constantly. However, these conversations cannot be our asking someone to

do something we want them to do. They're not coercive or sales conversations. We aren't asking someone to do us a favor.

No, what we're looking for is a sense of the values that animate the other person. We're trying to get a sense of who they are and what they care about. Any invitation to deeper engagement is simply a challenge to the person to live out their values in the public arena.

4. *Build.* To truly be part of a movement for justice, we need vehicles to channel our collective power. Nehemiah knew this. He connected with the people and then had a leadership meeting to connect the people to a shared campaign. Martin Luther King Jr. also knew this. When the bus boycott started, Black ministers and community leaders in Montgomery developed an organization to keep people moving in the same direction—the Montgomery Improvement Association. King served as president. When he decided to expand leadership throughout the South in early 1957, again civil rights activists built an organization: the Southern Christian Leadership Conference, which King led until his assassination. The student movement in the 1960s coalesced around a new organization called the Student Nonviolent Coordinating Committee.

In Cincinnati, as part of the AMOS Project, we are partners with a national organization, Faith in Action, that supports local and state work through partner organizations to move national justice efforts like access to health care, immigration reform, police reform, and voting rights.

Within these organizations, we also have the critical opportunity to build smaller teams inside our congregations. At Crossroads, back in 2016, we worked with some amazing leaders to build the UNDIVIDED Justice Team, which has worked for universal preschool and to address mass incarceration.

If you're in a congregation and want to get started, first look for what already might be moving in your community. What organizations are already connecting to channel power to bring about racial justice? Could a team from your church join with this broader effort?

One word of caution: as you connect with broader community efforts for justice, make sure that those most directly affected by the injustice are part of the organizing strategy. Remember the rights restoration campaign Troy joined? This was a coalition of churches with returning citizens, so the changes we were advancing were rooted in the power of faith and the power of those directly affected.

Sometimes you may need to consider creating a new vehicle in your community to advance racial justice. If this is a step you're considering, seek coaching from people in the work, like those at Faith in Action or other similar organizations. Also, as you begin to build, don't launch until those most affected are part of the process and strategy.

This work is vital if we are to be part of the restoration of God's world into the place God created it to be.

The prophet Isaiah says that when the people commit to justice, then

> your ancient ruins shall be rebuilt;
> > you shall raise up the foundations of many generations;
> you shall be called the repairer of the breach,
> > the restorer of streets to live in. (58:12)

This is the call for us: to restore streets to live in.

This is the plea in neighborhoods riddled with the scourge of gun violence: that they would find streets to live in.

This is the plea of immigrants trying to find their way in the US: that they can feel safe, that they would find streets to live in.

This is the plea of the people of East Liverpool, Ohio, in Appalachia, in the shadows of the nation's largest waste incinerator and with cancer rates far above the national average: that they would find streets to live in.

This is the plea of the people of Flint, Michigan, resiliently working to survive and thrive in the wake of a century of systemic racism and the horror of poisoned water: that they would find streets to live in.

This is the plea of returning citizens who are coming out of prison and have paid their debt to society and simply want to be treated as fully human: that they would find streets to live in.

Restoring of streets to live in says "No more" to any injustice that conspires against, wounds, and hurts Black, Indigenous, and People of Color. We're going to tear down that system and build something that enables everyone to have the chance to not only live but also thrive in the abundant life Jesus has promised us.

And when we look and see and act, God will hear our prayers. God will surround us, leading us forward and serving as our rear guard. And when we cry out, God will answer.

The calling and standard of living courageously should be no less than this: Can we repair divisions through deep personal and systemic work so the United States—for Black, Brown, and Indigenous people—is no longer the valley of the shadow of death but rather the land of the living? It demands confronting systemic injustice not just in words but in deeds.

Fan the Flame of Change

Howard Thurman, a great theologian and one of the spiritual mentors of the Civil Rights Movement, is famously reported to have said, "Don't ask yourself what the world needs. Ask yourself what makes you come alive, and go do that, because what the world needs is people who have come alive."

If you're coming alive to the call of Jesus to live out the words of Micah 6:8 and do justice, we want to fan that flame in you. Allow that to animate you, your apprenticeship to Jesus, and the life of your church. Allow that flame to help you garner the courage and commitment to stick with it when things are difficult. Surround yourself with other pastors and faith leaders who can strengthen you, stand in solidarity with you, and show the world what the church of Jesus looks like when we pursue justice. Because, as Dr. Cornel West said, "Justice is what love looks like in public."[2]

What makes you come alive?

EXAMINE YOUR STORY

1. Think about what comes to mind when you hear the word *power*. Is your first impression positive, negative, or neutral? Why?

2. If Jesus was pro-power rooted in love, how do you interpret our culture's use of power today? How do you interpret the church's use of power?

3. Do some research. What organizations in your church or community are focused on building power for racial change? How can you partner with them to bring healing and justice?

PART 6

RESOLVE

DO JUSTICE

5. RESTORE

6. RESOLVE—Committing to pursuing racial healing and justice by inviting others and developing leaders for lasting impact.

What happened next in the story of Nehemiah brings us through a complete evolution of the UNDIVIDED Circle. After Jerusalem's walls had been rebuilt, Nehemiah did something telling. "I gave my brother Hanani charge over Jerusalem, along with Hananiah the commander of the citadel, for he was a faithful man and feared God more than many" (Neh. 7:2).

Nehemiah gave them a few instructions, but before he left the city to return to Susa, he said, "Then my God put it into my mind to assemble the nobles and the officials and the people to be enrolled by genealogy" (v. 5).

This seemingly insignificant moment in Nehemiah's story is anything but. It was a moment of doing justice that cannot be overlooked. The wall was finished. Nehemiah had handed over the keys to his brother and empowered the people to care for their city, because he knew there was still work to be done. But before he left, God prompted Nehemiah to make a record of the people—all of them, the nobles and officials and the non-nobles and non-officials. Nehemiah knew titles wouldn't help in protecting the city, but resolving to do justice over time would require an effort from everyone.

Step Six: Resolve

We say the sixth step, not the final step, because the journey of bringing about racial healing, solidarity, and justice is one of continuous growth and repeated engagement. Fruitfulness in this work is fighting stagnancy and inviting and empowering others to join you. Jesus's commission to his followers was to make disciples: build powerful relationships, develop leaders, and expand the mission by empowering others.

Anyone who's ever attempted to read through the entire Bible knows that some of the most challenging parts are the chapters that contain long lists of names—like the list of names in Nehemiah 3 and 7.

While they may not be the most fascinating sections to read, they're powerful reminders that the movement of God goes forward, not mainly through extraordinary heroes but through ordinary people.

The names listed in Nehemiah are the names of ordinary people—people like you and me. Worse-for-wear, neglected, hardworking people who cared enough about their community to pick up a hammer and do something—do justice.

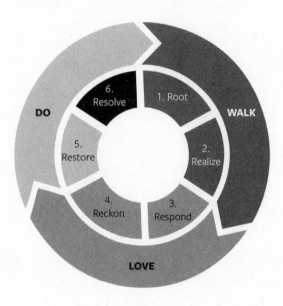

10 **Everyday Courage**

At the beginning of 2021, we both went on a trip to some of the key cities of the Civil Rights Movement in Alabama—Montgomery, Birmingham, and Selma. While in Selma, right after walking across the Edmund Pettus Bridge, we visited Brown Chapel, the church that served as the staging area for the historic marches that took place there. In front of the church is a bust of Dr. Martin Luther King Jr. and a dedication to some of those who gave their lives in the struggle for freedom, such as Jimmie Lee Jackson, who was born and lived in Marion, Alabama, a neighboring town to Selma.

What captured our attention, though, was another plaque to the right of the church, off in a corner easily overlooked by visitors. This plaque includes dozens of names of people who never had movies made about their lives or individual monuments erected in their honor. Yet without their commitment to do justice, there may well never have been a Voting Rights Act. Some of these names are listed as individuals, and some are captured as group names, such as "The Sewing Circle of Brown Chapel."

We would argue that as much as Dr. King and other visible leaders are worthy of the honor they've received for their leadership in the Civil Rights Movement, one thing that made the movement so effective was that there were heroes at every level.

Preschool Promise

As early as 2006, conversations began in Cincinnati about how to address a discouraging reality regarding education—students weren't succeeding in school. At the time, Ohio was ranked forty-two out of fifty states in the attainment of bachelor's degrees among its students. One of the outcomes of these conversations was the founding of the Strive Partnership, which developed goals to improve educational outcomes in the city.

Another sobering statistic was that 52 percent of children were living below the US poverty line, which at the time was second highest in the nation, behind only Detroit. We also learned that three out of every four Black children under the age of six were in a family living below the federal poverty line! Solving these long-standing problems would require creative solutions and the collective will of the community.

Because early childhood education plays an important role in a whole host of long-term outcomes, one idea proposed was the expansion of universal preschool in the city. This led to the creation of an initiative called the Preschool Promise, which focused on funding the expansion of quality preschool programs. Crossroads Church was one of the early adopters of the idea and helped fund the group's early efforts through our "Beans and Rice Campaign."

The idea of the campaign was this: church members spent a week living off a subsistence diet of just beans and rice (a regular diet for many people around the world) and took the difference in cost between that weekly food bill and what they'd normally spend and donated it as part of a combined gift to key organizations doing great work in our city. Preschool Promise was one of the initiatives Crossroads designated to receive funding from the campaign, and the money was used to expand access to preschool in one school for one year.

But we knew that a one-off gift or a boutique program wouldn't lead to systemic change or make a real dent in the daily lives of children and families struggling with poverty. We needed a systemic response, which sooner or later would require public dollars through new tax revenues.

We also did a lot of relationship building. We connected with dozens of churches. We built a platform of demands from the people of the city for implementing Preschool Promise that was anchored on four major pillars: Respect Every Child, Racial Equity, Only Good Jobs, and Family Voices at the Center.

Fast-forward to fall 2016. The Preschool Promise initiative was on the ballot in the form of a $48 million municipal levy to create the universal preschool program and support K–12 education. If implemented, taxes would go up by $278 for every $100,000 of the value of a home. This wasn't an easy sell, especially given the sharp racial divides in our city and who would be the primary beneficiaries of the levy.

While the general idea of expanding preschool for kids was something no one would argue against, would there be enough collective will in the community to actually follow through on that promise by agreeing to an increase in property taxes? We knew that if we were going to succeed, we had to develop leaders by getting them in motion and making sure they saw this as their struggle.

LivingUNDIVIDED alums were determined to do their part. With the help of the AMOS Project (which was being led by Troy at the time), we rolled up our sleeves and went to work. Over the months leading up to the fall 2016 election, more than 250 LivingUNDIVIDED participants worked over 500 volunteer shifts, knocking on doors and making phone calls to convince the constituency to vote yes for the levy.

Chuck even became one of the spokespersons for the campaign, filming commercials and making other appearances. It was the first time Chuck had ever publicly campaigned for a ballot issue. The broader coalition of faith, business, education, and other civic leaders gave us hope that this could pass. However, negative ads and a well-organized opposition began to emerge, and by the time we got to election night, we were nervous.

The final result was that the citizens of Cincinnati voted for a critical win for racial equity and justice. The levy passed by a twenty-four-point margin, garnering over 62 percent of the vote. In our city, people were voting for children. Cincinnati decided to invest in the future of Black and Brown children.

Recall the words of Dr. King about love and power: "Power at its best is love implementing the demands of justice, and justice at its best is love correcting everything that stands against love."[1]

In the years leading up to the historic passage of that levy, there was a very intentional effort to build power. The coalition behind the levy didn't consist only of the political and economic elites in our community. There were parents, day care owners, and many blue-collar workers with a vested interest in bettering the lives of their children. They weren't on the outside looking in. The AMOS Project leaders, in fact, had publicly made themselves accountable to this constituency and what they wanted to see happen with this levy.

It was a powerful coalition, and it was rooted in love. Ascribing worth to working parents. Ascribing worth to teachers and educators both in public schools and in small childcare centers. Ascribing worth to the 52 percent of children living in poverty.

It was power at its best implementing the demands of justice in education, and it was justice at its best correcting everything that stands against love.

I-C-N-U

Dave Ferguson, who wrote the foreword for this book, is committed to the development of the future leaders of the church. In a book he coauthored titled *Hero Maker*, he talks about the five practices of a hero maker, a leader who operates with the belief that "my fruit grows on other people's trees."[2]

He talks in the book about how the four most important letters in the English language are I-C-N-U, short for "I see in you." It's the practice of calling out the gifts and talents of another person and empowering them to use who God made them to be in order to have a positive impact in the world.[3]

As we build power, this is how we invite others into greater leadership in the public arena in the fight for justice. We're convinced God has already planted and nurtured all the people, energy, gifts, and talents needed for an UNDIVIDED movement. We see that in you and believe it's why you were drawn to read this book. Our invitation is for you to embrace your God-given power and invite others into this journey.

Power Building

I (Troy) saw this power when I got involved in an effort to stop the deportation of Bernard Pastor back in 2010. Bernard Pastor was eighteen years old and working at a Chick-fil-A on the north side of Cincinnati. He's a devout Christian and the son of a pastor of a largely undocumented congregation. He decided one day to deliver some Bibles to a few of his coworkers. On the way there, he got into a fender bender. The wreck wasn't his fault, but because Bernard didn't have a driver's license and was undocumented, the police fast-tracked him for deportation.

Bernard had come to this country when he was three years old. His family, along with his uncle's family, had fled religious persecution in Guatemala. Bernard's uncle's family was granted religious asylum, and they're all US citizens today. Bernard's family, just because they were in a different court at a different time on a different day with a different judge, was denied religious asylum. But Bernard's father felt like he had been called to stay in the United States, so Bernard grew up here, finishing in the top five of his class. And yet, after that fender bender, he was on the fast track to deportation.

A number of community and faith leaders began to raise their voices, and Bernard was released in December 2010 on the night before the DREAM Act vote at the US Senate. The White House and others intervened on Bernard's behalf.

Bernard Pastor and I flew to DC, and that morning we happened upon our Ohio senator George Voinovich, a longtime opponent of the DREAM Act. The senator said quickly, "I'm not voting for that bill." For most of our conversation, Voinovich refused to look Bernard in the eye. Later that day, the DREAM Act was defeated.

After this crushing defeat, I was invited into the bowels of the Capitol building, surrounded by nearly three hundred Dreamers who had just lost a fight for their lives on the Senate floor. I'm not sure I've ever been in such a sacred space. Tears flowed freely, including mine. Then leaders began to share. Some expressed deep disappointment and sadness. Others shared righteous anger. But undergirding every word was a fierce determination, a firm belief that the struggle was far from over.

They leaned on God, believing justice was possible. They embodied resolve and made a commitment to continue to build power and grow their movement. So it was no surprise to me that just eighteen months later, the people in that room built a movement so strong that they pushed then-president Obama to issue the executive order for Deferred Action for Childhood Arrivals (DACA), which remains in effect years later.

This is the type of power building, rooted in calling out the best in one another, that's possible. Nehemiah knew this and called out the best in the people of Jerusalem until the city was restored.

We invite you, in the same way Nehemiah invited his people, to join us in the work of healing the wounds of racial injustice and cultivating equitable relationships, institutions, and communities where all people can flourish. And don't let the flow end with you. Invite others into the work alongside you.

Achmed and Mike

In the summer of 2021, we (Chuck and Troy) walked into a completely foreign environment together. We entered a room of about five hundred people, mostly police officers and their families, and all but five of the attendees were White.

During the ceremony, police and other first responders were recognized in a broad range of categories. There was even a German shepherd who won Canine of the Year!

One of the attendees of Color was Achmed Beighle, who, along with police chief Mike Mills, had invited us to the banquet. Achmed, an alumnus of LivingUNDIVIDED, received the Citizen Recognition Award. Being in that room to honor Achmed was one of the highlights of our year, because his journey to the podium was the embodiment of what it means to live undivided.

The power of Achmed and Mike's story is rooted in authenticity and relationship with each other that served as a catalyst for positive impact in their community.

The ground rules of LivingUNDIVIDED include giving grace and taking risks. When Achmed, his wife, and the others in his mixed-race group experienced LivingUNDIVIDED, they leaned into their new relationships in courageous ways and developed deeper friendships over the following years.

Achmed grew up in Suriname in South America and lives in a mostly White suburb of Cincinnati. At first glance, his town feels distant from the racial tensions that boiled over around the nation in 2020. Still, when Achmed watched the death of George Floyd on the news, he experienced a mix of grief and internal tension. Upon reflection, Achmed realized he couldn't shake the urge to invite his local police chief out to lunch to talk about what happened to George Floyd. To be clear, Achmed didn't know his local police chief personally, so you might imagine how awkward it'd be to just reach out to him and say, "Hi, you don't know me, but I'm a Black citizen in the township, and I want to take you to lunch."

After the unshakable urge to act didn't leave him, Achmed reached out to police chief Mike Mills. Chief Mills, who grew up in a low-income, all-White neighborhood, cares deeply about people. This concern led him to a career in law enforcement and eventually to become the Chief of the Miami Township Police Department. Chief Mills, like Achmed, was deeply troubled by what happened to George Floyd and how it impacted not just Black citizens' view of police, but all residents of his township. When Achmed invited Mike to lunch, Mike agreed.

Achmed shared with Mike how he was feeling following Floyd's murder and that he wanted to understand what Mike was doing to ensure something like that never happened in their community. Chief Mills had answers: training, body cams, and open communication with citizens like Achmed. These were all good things Achmed was happy to hear about. Since he had already taken the leap of faith to invite Mike to lunch, Achmed followed God's prompting to make another invitation. He told Mike how his experience with UNDIVIDED had led to deep, cross-racial friendships that he and his wife wouldn't have otherwise.

Then Achmed asked Mike an intriguing question: "What if we bring the UNDIVIDED experience to our township and do it with police in your department and Black citizens in the community?" Mike said yes.

A few weeks later, we found ourselves on a Zoom call with Achmed and Mike, discussing how this could happen. We told them both that it would require them to recruit a diverse group, and people would need to be willing to give grace and take risks.

These two amazing leaders went into recruitment mode and pulled together a diverse cohort both racially and vocationally. During the first night of the virtual experience, there was palpable tension. A few of the officers had the "thin blue line" flag as their backdrop, and it was obviously making some of the Black citizens on the call a bit uncomfortable. We could also tell by the longer-than-usual silence after open-ended questions that the officers and the citizens were feeling each other out.

Then it happened.

We'll never forget the moment when both Achmed and Chief Mills shared vulnerably about their thoughts and feelings coming into the experience. They talked about their lunch, about the honest questions they both were asking. They also talked about the commitment they had made to each other to partner together to build solidarity and understanding so Miami Township would be an exemplary community that didn't shy away from these challenges but leaned in with courage and hope. These two leaders went first, and after that the group began to open up and step fully into the experience. Over their time together, they got honest and fostered deeper empathy and understanding of what it might be like to walk a mile in one another's shoes.

In the last week, each participant had a chance to reflect on what they were leaving behind and what they wanted to take away from the experience. It was powerful to hear officers and citizens share what they had learned and their commitment to each other to continue to do the challenging work of living undivided in their community.

One of the Black women in the group had a powerful revelation over the weeks. When it was her turn to share, everyone listened closely because she had not been one to mince words! Her reflection was that she said yes to doing the experience "to set these White police officers straight!" She went on to say that over the time of getting to know the officers beyond just the uniform, she realized that when she had seen a police officer before, she'd only seen the uniform and not the person. She proclaimed that she wanted to leave behind her tendency to judge a book by its cover and instead continue building relationships with the officers beyond the seven sessions. The group has continued to connect through cookouts and community events.

This group is now furthering an ongoing commitment to live undivided in their community. They've done joint projects together and continue to foster broader connections. Their work together has drawn the attention of other police departments and even other facets of the criminal legal system, and there's growing interest for others to experience the same journey that's strengthening the bonds between the police and the citizens in this community.

This story is a reminder of the power of a single yes. Achmed said yes to the prompting to reach out to Mike Mills. Mike said yes to engaging Achmed in a friendship and in leveraging his leadership to bring even more people together in his community. We believe God honors the power of a single yes.

As you conclude this journey, reflect on what you've experienced while reading this book. What do you want to leave behind or stop doing as you commit to live undivided? Maybe it's a fear of saying or doing the wrong thing, or maybe it's withholding forgiveness from someone for the way they've wounded you in the past. What do you want to take with you for the journey ahead? Maybe it's an appreciation of our shared history or remembering the titans who've led well on race out of a commitment to be like Jesus in the public square. Hopefully you'll reject powerlessness and join with others to advance racial healing, solidarity, and justice in your community. Finally, where are you at in the UNDIVIDED Circle? How will you take your next step? Whatever you answer to the question, we believe the change you want to see begins with a single yes.

EPILOGUE

A Call to Living Undivided

It Starts with You

> He has shown you, O mortal, what is good.
>   And what does the LORD require of you?
> To act justly and to love mercy
>   and to walk humbly with your God.
>   Micah 6:8 (NIV)

This entire book has been written to encourage you to walk humbly, love mercy, and do justice. And to see that by doing so, God can use you in the work of racial healing and justice.

It starts with you.

It starts with you choosing courage over fear.

It starts with you choosing love over indifference.

It starts with you allowing God's redeeming power to lead you away from stagnancy toward loving action.

As you read this book, we pray that something was spurred in your heart and spirit. If so, it's vital that you don't stagnate but continue to flow toward how God is calling you to live undivided.

We invite you to be part of a growing community of followers of Jesus who are committed to loving courageously for racial healing and justice. A community rooted in the following core values:

Jesus. We are committed followers of Jesus who are grounded in love, guided by Scripture, committed to spiritual formation, led by the Spirit, and passionate about the church.

Investment. We commit to knowledge and action, internally and externally, for racial solidarity and justice.

Courage. We stand firmly in our convictions and lean humbly into our concessions.

Joy. Our priority of cultivating joy helps our souls thrive.

Humility. We serve our team and submit to this mission with purpose.

UNDIVIDED is not a hopeful hypothetical; it's a concrete way to bring people together and catalyze them to be change agents. And we believe it starts with you.

Use the QR code on the next page to connect with us. We would love to partner with you and help you take your next step.

Every LivingUNDIVIDED group ends with the same commissioning and prayer moment. While we hope you'll engage with us beyond this book, we want to commission you and leave you with a blessing as we come to the end of our learning journey together in this book.

A Prayer for Living Undivided

Before you ever picked up this book, we and our entire team were praying for you. This prayer reflects our desire for you as you answer the call to live undivided:

> *We commission you as ministers of reconciliation for the kingdom of God in the name of Jesus Christ and in the power of the Holy Spirit.*
>
> *You are empowered by Jesus to walk into places of division and bring unity. You are equipped to bring empathy where there have been only echo chambers. You are connected to a community of reconcilers who stand with you to bring God's love and justice to relationships, neighborhoods, workplaces, school campuses, churches, cities, and a nation so that there's more unity, more hope, more forgiveness, more redemption, and more of the kingdom of God here on earth.*
>
> *And finally, you are strengthened to see fruit as you faithfully pursue this calling in the name of our reconciling God and King, Jesus Christ.*
>
> *AMEN.*

Let's Come Alive!

We believe you are called to live undivided, and we can help you come alive to this calling. Connect with us personally at this QR code:

ACKNOWLEDGMENTS

We want to thank our wives, Amanda and Maria, for being supportive throughout this process and also for serving as endless sources of wise counsel.

To our kids, Jacob, Emma, Ellie, Nathan, Samuel, and Isabel: You give us hope that the future will be better than today.

To our parents: We love and thank you for your constant support. Each of you has been a source of love and grace to us, and we know Jesus better because of you.

Family and friends: Thank you for all the ways you encouraged us and stretched us to find our voices in this important work.

To Holly: You were an amazing writing partner. Thank you for going all in and being willing to collaborate with us to bring life to this book.

To the founding team of UNDIVIDED: Lynn, Charla, Justin, Paul, Kathy, Beverly, and Kristie. Lots of creativity, time, hard work, passionate conversations, and Jason's Deli birthed LivingUNDIVIDED. Thank you for your Spirit-inspired commitment to racial healing, solidarity, and justice.

To Brittany, Courtney, Natalie, Morgan, and our entire team: Each of you put your heart and energy into creating the culture from which this book could emerge. Your feedback was pivotal. What we are building together now is powerful, and we are far better leaders and people because we're on this journey with you. The best is yet to come!

To our board: Thank you for your wisdom, encouragement, and commitment to the ongoing work of UNDIVIDED. You are all amazing people and amazing leaders.

To our UNDIVIDED alums and partners: Hub team members, certified facilitators, and program alums, you represent courage and love in action. Let's continue to embrace the flow of racial healing and justice together for a better future.

To Crossroads Church: From the board to the staff to the entire Crossroads community, you've been a spiritual home and a source of strength and support for over two decades. Let's keep changing the world!

To Faith in Action: Alvin, Michael-Ray, Phyllis, Andrea, Juard, and so many others, you have shaped our commitment to racial justice and our strong conviction that doing justice demands action.

To those who have supported our growth in the work for racial healing, solidarity, and justice: Ray McMillan, Wilmot Allen, Damon Lynch III, Michael McBride, Iris Roley, Chris Beard, Kirk Noden, DaMareo Cooper, Joy Cushman, Marshall Ganz, Hahrie Han, Elizabeth McKenna, Jerry Culbreth, Dwight Wilkins, Brian Tome, Chuck Moore, Paul Heagen, Harvey Young, Lisa Sharon Harper, Mae Cannon, Brenda Salter McNeil, Soong-Chan Rah, Doran Schrantz, David Bailey, Andrew Hanauer, Steve Haas, John Kingston, Tim and Joyce Dalrymple, Elizabeth Hopkins, Scott Reed, Chris Heiert, Dude Group, and the Running Group. Thank you.

To the team at Baker and the Fedd Agency: Thank you for your trust and support throughout this project. We're grateful to be in partnership with you.

To everyone who contributed by sharing their personal story in this book: Carolyn Heck, Taisha Rojas-Parker, Vince Lam, Tamika Decatur, John Tanner, Mary Jackson, Rev. Damon Lynch III, Gene Mays, Eric Dorsey, Brian Dershaw, Mario Stuckey, Achmed Beighle, and Mike Mills. Thank you for the generosity of spirit you showed in allowing us to include your stories in the book. We are inspired by you and can't wait for others to be inspired by your stories too.

NOTES

Introduction

1. Eminem, "Lose Yourself," track 1 on *8 Mile: Music from and Inspired by the Motion Picture*, Shady Records, 2002, compact disc.

2. Hahrie Han, Elizabeth McKenna, Michelle Oyakawa, *Prisms of the People, Power, and Organizing in Twenty-First-Century America* (Chicago: University of Chicago Press, 2021), 16.

3. Takim Williams, "#InContext: Cornel West," Human Trafficking Institute, accessed May 12, 2023, https://traffickinginstitute.org/incontext-cornel-west/.

Part 1 Root

1. Lisa Sharon Harper, *Fortune: How Race Broke My Family and the World and How to Repair It All* (Grand Rapids: Brazos, 2022), 31.

Chapter 2 Troy's Story

1. Lisa Cozzens, "The Murder of Emmett Till," Watson.org, last modified June 29, 1998, http://www.watson.org/~lisa/blackhistory/early-civilrights/emmett.html.

Chapter 3 Hope in History

1. "Second Baptist Church," New Richmond on the Ohio Underground Railroad Tour, accessed May 12, 2023, http://newrichmondugrrtour.weebly.com/second-baptist-church.html#:~:text=In%201857%20Boone%20was%20a,by%20more%20than%2050%20years.

2. Lisa Smith, "New Richmond's Rich Black History Connects to the Underground Railroad," WCPO 9 News, February 6, 2020, https://www.wcpo.com/news/local-news/hamilton-county/cincinnati/new-richmonds-rich-black-history-connects-to-the-underground-railroad.

3. Shannon H. Wilson, *Berea College: An Illustrated History* (Lexington: University Press of Kentucky, 2006), 1.

4. Martin Luther King Jr., "MIA Mass Meeting at Holt Street Baptist Church," December 5, 1955, Montgomery, AL, https://kinginstitute.stanford.edu/king-papers/documents/mia-mass-meeting-holt-street-baptist-church.

5. Troy Jackson, *Becoming King: Martin Luther King Jr. and the Making of a National Leader* (Lexington: University Press of Kentucky, 2008).

6. Cesar Chavez, *Letter from Cesar Chavez to Friends regarding Peregrinacion*, 1966, accessed March 24, 2023, https://libraries.ucsd.edu/farmworker movement/essays/essays/MillerArchive/016%20Letter%20From%20Cesar% 20Chavez%20To%20Friends.pdf.

7. Chavez, *Letter from Cesar Chavez.*

8. Dolores Huerta, National Farm Workers Association march and rally, speech, April 10, 1966, Sacramento, CA.

Chapter 4 Stagnant Roots

1. *Shelley v. Kraemer* (1948).

2. Zane L. Miller, "History and the Politics of Community Change in Cincinnati," *The Public Historian 5*, no. 4 (1983): 17–35.

3. Motoko Rich, Amanda Cox, and Matthew Bloch, "Money, Race, and Success: How Your School District Compares," *New York Times*, April 29, 2016, https://www.nytimes.com/interactive/2016/04/29/upshot/money-race -and-success-how-your-school-district-compares.html.

4. *DeRolph v. State* (2002), https://www.supremecourt.ohio.gov/rod/docs /pdf/0/2002/2002-Ohio-6750.pdf.

5. Carl Schoettler, "For Black Steel Men, the Living Wasn't Easy Documentary: African-Americans Working in the Industry Not So Long Ago Found That Discrimination Was Part of the Job. Three Who Were There Tell about It," *Baltimore Sun*, February 2, 1998, https://www.baltimoresun.com/news/bs-xpm -1998-02-02-1998033014-story.html.

6. Michelle Alexander, *The New Jim Crow: Mass Incarceration in the Age of Colorblindness* (New York: The New Press, 2010), 26.

7. Andrew R. Highsmith and Ansley T. Erickson, "Segregation as Splitting, Segregation as Joining: Schools, Housing, and the Many Modes of Jim Crow," *American Journal of Education* 121, no. 4 (August 2015): 582, https:// doi.org/10.1086/681942.

8. Andrew Highsmith, *Demolition Means Progress: Flint, Michigan, and the Fate of the American Metropolis*, Historical Studies of Urban America (Chicago: University of Chicago Press, 2015), 286.

Chapter 5 Two Empowering Commitments

1. Albert Hirschman, *Exit, Voice, and Loyalty: Responses to Decline in Firms, Organizations, and States* (Boston: Harvard University Press, 1970).

Chapter 6 The Power of Community

1. United States Census Bureau, "2020 Census Statistics Highlight Local Population Changes and Nation's Racial and Ethnic Diversity," news release no. CB21-CN.55, August 12, 2021, https://www.census.gov/newsroom/press -releases/2021/population-changes-nations-diversity.html.

Chapter 7 The Faithful Path

1. Martin Luther King Jr., "It's Hard to Be a Christian," sermon, February 5, 1956, Montgomery, AL, https://kinginstitute.stanford.edu/king-papers/documents/its-hard-be-christian.

2. "State of Black Cincinnati 2015: Two Cities" (Cincinnati: Greater Cincinnati Urban League, 2015), http://homecincy.org/wp-content/uploads/2015/09/The-State-of-Black-Cincinnati-2015_Two-Cities.pdf.

3. "Dr. William Holmes Borders Gives Resume of Negro History in His Poem That Will Eventually Become a Classic in American History and Literature," *Pittsburgh Courier*, February 20, 1943, https://www.newspapers.com/clip/1206542/i-am-somebody-by-dr-william-holmes/.

4. "I Am Somebody," *Sesame Street*, aired May 1972, YouTube video, posted by LittleJerryFan 92, July 1, 2007, https://www.youtube.com/watch?v=iTB1h18bHlY.

Chapter 8 Power Supply

1. Martin Luther King Jr., "'The Most Durable Power,' excerpt from Sermon at Dexter Avenue Baptist Church on 6 November 1956," in *The Papers of Martin Luther King, Jr.: Advocate of the Social Gospel, September 1948–March 1963*, eds. Clayborne Carson, Susan Carson, Susan Englander, Troy Jackson, and Gerald R. Smith, vol. 6 (Oakland: University of California Press, 2007), 303.

2. Martin Luther King Jr., "Where Do We Go from Here?," speech, Atlanta, GA, August 16, 1967, https://kinginstitute.stanford.edu/where-do-we-go-here.

3. Martin Luther King Jr., "Speeches on the Steps of the Alabama State Capitol," speech, March 25, 1965, Montgomery, AL, https://digital.libraries.psu.edu/digital/collection/rabin/id/2397.

4. Martin Luther King Jr., "Our God Is Marching On," speech, March 25, 1965, Montgomery, AL, https://kinginstitute.stanford.edu/our-god-marching.

5. E. W. Kenworthy, "Johnson Signs Voting Rights Bill, Orders Immediate Enforcement; 4 Suits Will Challenge Poll Tax; Capital Is Scene," *New York Times*, August 7, 1965, https://archive.nytimes.com/www.nytimes.com/library/national/race/080765race-ra.html.

Chapter 9 What Does the Lord Require of You?

1. Charles Payne, "Ella Baker and Models of Change," *Signs: Journal of Women in Culture and Society* 14, no. 4 (Summer 1989): 897.

2. Cornel West (@CornelWest), "Justice is what love looks like in public. Tenderness is what love looks like in private. This is beautiful," Twitter, October 17, 2018, 11:41 a.m., https://twitter.com/cornelwest/status/1052585306916974592.

Chapter 10 Everyday Courage

1. Martin Luther King Jr., "Where Do We Go from Here?," speech, Atlanta, GA, August 16, 1967, https://kinginstitute.stanford.edu/where-do-we-go-here.

2. Dave Ferguson, *Hero Maker* (Grand Rapids: Zondervan, 2018), 169.

3. Ferguson, *Hero Maker*.

ABOUT THE AUTHORS

CHUCK MINGO is the cofounder of UNDIVIDED, a nonprofit organization built to unite and ignite people for racial justice through programming that helps participants experience life-changing moments of racial healing. With his passion for justice and racial reconciliation, Chuck has transformed a congregational training into a national movement with hub cities emerging throughout the country. Chuck's leadership has inspired and mobilized thousands from diverse backgrounds around the nation and even the world.

In addition to leading Courageous Love, Chuck teaches and consults for churches and organizations around the country on a variety of topics related to race relations and racial justice.

For thirteen years, Chuck has served as a teaching pastor at one of the largest churches in America, Crossroads Church. Prior to being a pastor, Chuck spent nine years in the corporate world at Procter & Gamble. He earned his bachelor's in business administration at Duquesne University. Chuck is married with three children and calls Cincinnati, Ohio, home.

Connect with Chuck:

www.ChuckMingo.com

@ChuckDMingo

@ChuckMingo

@ChuckMingo

TROY JACKSON is cofounder and part of the core team of UNDIVIDED. Dr. Jackson has been involved in community organizing over the past decade and continues to work for a pathway to citizenship for the undocumented, an end to mass incarceration and the criminalization of Black and Brown communities, and universal preschool. From 2014 to 2018, Troy served as the executive director of the AMOS Project, a faith-based organizing effort that regularly engages more than fifty congregations in Greater Cincinnati to work for racial and economic justice. Troy now leads evangelical engagement for Faith in Action, a national faith organizing network that works to dismantle systems of injustice.

Troy is a coauthor of *Forgive Us: Confessions of a Compromised Faith*, which explores the historic sins of the American church. Troy earned his MDiv at Princeton Theological Seminary and a PhD in United States history from the University of Kentucky. Troy's book *Becoming King: Martin Luther King Jr. and the Making of a National Leader* explores the critical role the grassroots Montgomery movement played in the development of King. Troy's other publications include his work as an editor on *The Papers of Martin Luther King, Jr., Volume VI: Advocate of the Social Gospel*. Troy and his wife, Amanda, live in Cincinnati.

Connect with Troy:

- @Troy.Jackson.3954
- @TroyJackson1968
- @TTJackson